ADVANCE PRAISE

"Teaching is hard work! Some days are really good, but then there are others that are more of a challenge. We all need extra encouragement and inspiration at times, and Joan Tidwell's book provides inspiration and encouragement on timely topics for teachers of all grade levels and all levels of experience. I cannot recommend this book enough!"

—CHET V., classroom teacher

"Salve to a teacher's heart."

—VICKI L., math coach

"Joan Tidwell speaks from years of experience and godly wisdom to touch your teacher-heart, no matter what state yours is currently in. Don't miss out on the opportunity to laugh, cry, and pray while diving into this amazing devotional."

—MANDY M., instructional coach

The Heart of a Teacher

Weekly Devotions for the School Year

Joan Tidwell

Cover design: Kristen Ingebretson
Editing: Natalie Hanemann
Typesetter: Roseanna White

ISBN: TK (print)
ISBN: TK (digital)
Printed in the United States of America.

Dedicated to my two favorite teachers:

To Barbara, my sister in heaven. You were a master teacher, and you set the bar high for the teachers in our family. We never tire of hearing stories from former students of your life-changing influence. Your teacher's heart continues to inspire and encourage as your influence is woven into the pages of these devotions.

To Janelle, my sister on earth. Your determination to finish college at fifty-seven after a successful career of teaching preschool inspired us all to never stop learning and growing and following our dreams. I'm always amazed at the creative ways you make learning fun and meaningful for your students, and I learn something new about teaching every time we talk.

I love you both.

"Oh, we ain't got a barrel of money, maybe we're ragged and funny, but we travel along, singing a song side by side."
—Harry M. Woods, "Side by Side"

Contents

Introduction

I retired from nearly forty years in education in 2014. It wasn't something I planned or expected, but over my career I always prayed that God would let me know when it was time to stop, and He did.

Just months before my decision to retire, our family experienced the unexpected and devastating deaths of my older sister and two close members of my husband's family. Still broken by the deaths of our infant grandson and my mother only a few short years before that, our family needed to heal, and my presence was needed at home. The decision to leave my beloved profession was a good one for many reasons but leaving behind my life's work proved more difficult than I imagined. The layers of grief made for a very difficult season.

When my heart is heavy and my body needs refreshing, I head to the beach. My intentions for that particular beach trip were to get enough sun and ocean air to soothe my aching heart and to get a plan for moving forward. I got on the beach early that first morning while my family slept. I just wanted to sit in undisturbed silence and imagine the waves washing my grief out to sea. But God had bigger plans for me that day.

As soon as I sat in my beach chair and took that first sip of Diet Coke, I caught sight of a nearby family out enjoying the early-morning ocean waves. The father's towering height caught my attention first, but my gaze stayed on him because of how engaged he was, playing and laughing with his three young children, obviously delighted to be in their presence.

I was particularly captivated by the devotion he showed his youngest child, a little girl just old enough to toddle by herself. At first, he held her hand and walked her to the edge of the water. When she'd discovered the joy of the waves and began to explore the beauty around her, he released her hand but remained in rescuing distance. Sometimes he stood behind her with his hand ready to scoop her up if necessary, and sometimes he simply stepped in front of her so she couldn't go beyond the limits of her own safety. But always, he encouraged and enjoyed her every attempt to conquer the waves.

At one point, in her fascination with the ocean, she ventured out a little too far. He spoke her name, calling her back to the safety of his protection. The most tender moment happened when at the peak of feeling tired, scared, and a little overwhelmed, she reached out her arms for her daddy. He picked her up, held her close, and pointed out to the ocean. I couldn't hear his words, but I could imagine he was showing her how, from his perspective, the waves didn't look as scary and the possibilities for ocean adventure were exciting and endless. They stood there for the longest moment with her cheek resting against his, looking out at the horizon together. She looked safe and peaceful in her father's arms, and the look of love and pride on his face reflected his total delight in the child he held so close.

It was a mesmerizing few moments for me as I casually enjoyed the dynamic of that father and his kids. And then it hit me. I had just witnessed the most profound reminder of my heavenly Father's heart for me! "I will be a Father to you, and you will be my sons and daughters, says the Lord Almighty" (2 Cor 6:18). I always knew my Father loved me, but after seeing that Scripture verse play out for me like a movie, I understood more fully what that love looks like.

This book of devotions was borne out of my experience on the beach that day. Seeing God as a loving, engaged Father who delights in me, who never leaves me alone, and who gently picks me up when life makes standing on my own too difficult changed my perspective and launched me on an unexpected journey. Over the next two years, God would not only heal my heart, but infuse it with a renewed passion for my profession.

At the core of my being, I will forever be a teacher. I love the electric atmosphere inside of schools. I love the immense potential to make a global impact planted deep within every student who walks through the doors. I love the rhythm of school, how we can leave behind the failures and regrets from the year before and look to the endless possibilities in the year to come. I love the kids with their enthusiasm, their energy, and their courage to walk into a new class each year and put their trust in a stranger.

I have a special love for teachers, though. You are the heart of the school. You are the warriors. You have a passion to make a difference, and you work long hours and put your heart on the line every day. Somehow, you manage the demands of the curriculum, the needs of the students, the mandates of administration, the expectations of parents, the attempts of politicians, and the ups and downs of culture to shape the minds and hearts of those who will, in a few short years, make decisions that impact us all. Your work is nothing short of heroic.

But heroes don't always have it easy, do they? I know you often experience mind-numbing exhaustion. I know at times the mountains of demands on your time and energy leave you feeling defeated. I know the intensity of expectations for working miracles often leaves you wondering how long you can keep up this pace. I know discouragement sometimes creeps into your heart, filling you with questions about the value of your work.

My hope is that this little book will help you to experience what I felt on the beach when God showed me that picture of His love. I want you to be encouraged by the image of God as our Father, completely present, walking with us through this crazy teaching adventure, cheering us on through failures and successes. I want you to find strength in knowing that our Father is so attentive to our needs that He graciously prevents us from venturing beyond the limits of His protection. I want you to revel in His invitation to reach out our arms to Him in prayer when we need His reassurance. I want you to feel His delight as He cradles us against Him. And I want you to feel renewed in your own passion for teaching as God lifts you up past the waves and points out the endless possibilities you have to touch His world through the work you do every day.

These devotions are divided into five categories:

1. Reclaiming Significance: What I Do Matters

2. Restoring Peace and Joy: God Is the Source

3. Declaring Victory: Trusting God's Power in Difficult Times

4. Choosing Empowerment: Knowing What I Have Control Over

5. Pleading for God's Help: Seeking Divine Guidance and Intervention

The book is designed for you to read one devotion per week, allowing time for prayer and meditation on the message and Scripture verses the rest of the week. While there are typically thirty-six weeks of school, I only included twenty-six entries to accommodate school breaks and the first and last few weeks of school when time is short. Some topics will speak to your heart so personally that you may choose to spend more than one week meditating on God's message to you.

While you can read and pray on each devotion in your own quiet time, they are also designed to be used in a small group meeting once a week. The *Reflections* section of each entry has three discussion points to spark personal reflections and/or community discussion.

At the end of each weekly devotion are Scripture selections. My hope is that you will copy them, memorize them, put them on post-it notes on your computer, clip them in the potty ads in the teacher's bathrooms. Please read them and let God's Word speak to you. He, of course, says it so much better than I can!

The devotions do not need to be read in order; however, I do suggest reading "Chosen" first because it sets the tone for the rest of the devotions. After that, you can read straight through or pick and choose from the table of contents, depending on your heart-needs that week. My prayer is that

God will use each devotion to provide encouragement and hope at your exact point of need.

While all names and identifying characteristics have been changed to respect privacy, all of the narratives in the devotions are based on my own experiences or those of colleagues. Some are composites of many people or experiences. My goal is for no single person to see himself/herself in any particular devotion, but for us all to identify with the struggles and celebrations embedded in each narrative.

The stories I've included are clearly from an elementary school setting because that is where I taught and led. If you are a middle or high school teacher, my hope is that the promises of God brought to life through the experiences I share will transcend grade levels.

I am far from being a model Christian. In fact, I have made huge mistakes many more times than I've done it right. I am a recipient of the infinite and loving grace of God. He has picked me up, forgiven me, counseled me, healed me, walked with me, and loved me through many seasons of life. I wrote these devotions not as a testimony to anything I've done but to point you to the living God who wants to do the same for you.

My prayer for you as you read the devotions is that you allow the image of God as a loving, engaged Father to captivate your heart. Don't forget you're where He wants you to be…so try to enjoy it…have some fun. Laugh and play and lose yourself in the beauty of teaching. When a new challenge comes and you need to step out of your comfort zone, try to embrace it. Remember that your Father stands always close enough to rescue you when you need His strong hands. And when your adventure starts to look a little scary, reach your arms up to Him in prayer. Let Him lift you above the waves and show you His eternal vantage point. Then rest awhile with your cheek against His, feel the warmth of His love as He holds you in His arms. Allow Him to fill your heart with new strength and passion.

Thank you for what you do every day. Thank you for the sacrifices you make. Thank you for the possibilities you see in every child. And thank you for making our future brighter because you are willing to teach our children. Thank you for your heart to teach.

You are my heroes.

Part One
RECLAIMING SIGNIFICANCE

WHAT I DO MATTERS

Chosen
HANDPICKED TO TEACH

My daughter was six months old when a group of friends invited me to a weekend in the mountains. I looked forward to time with grown-ups, but more than that, I was excited to get four hours alone in my car for some quiet time to think. My expectations for a peaceful drive, though, were interrupted as my thoughts swirled around the enormous assignment of motherhood. What if I got it wrong? What if I messed her up? How would I know what to do? Question after question invaded my thoughts, and suddenly I was overwhelmed by the fear that I would be a terrible mother.

Crying and praying, I scribbled the questions that came pouring from my soul onto the white McDonald's sack left over from lunch. After nearly three hours of pouring my heart out to God, I pulled into a rest stop to take a break and pull myself together before meeting my friends. I picked up that sack of fearful questions to look at them again and as I did, a beautiful peace settled around me, and I felt God's answer to all my questions with one whisper to my heart, *"You're the mother I chose for her."* Three days later, on the trip back home, the questions that had sparked so much fear became lines in a lullaby for my baby girl. The last verse will always be my favorite:

The answers, my darling, I don't have them all.
At times when I rock you, I feel very small.
But then God whispers to me in a voice soft and warm,
"You're the mother I chose for that child in your arms."

I was *chosen*! Handpicked by God to be the mother of this miracle. This changed the way I looked at motherhood, and I knew deep in my heart that God would equip me to be the mother my daughter needed.

I returned to teaching when she was three. Even though I had eleven years' experience, that first year back stretched me to my limit. A new school, new curriculum, challenging behaviors, and the unfamiliar struggle of balancing parenting and working birthed in me new questions about my calling. *How can I possibly do everything I'm being asked to do? How do I balance it all? Do I have what it takes to do this? Is it even worth the hours and the tears?*

I struggled with those questions for the next ten years as a classroom teacher, a central office consultant, and, finally, as a principal. Until one day that same daughter who had listened to those questions through the lens of her lullaby, looked me in the eye and said, "You know, Mom, God chose you for this job."

Dear teachers, I want you to know that you are chosen too. You were handpicked to teach by our Creator. Think about it. God lovingly and thoughtfully created you. You are His masterpiece, His miracle, His handiwork. As He formed you, He considered the gifts, the desires, and the character that would be part of your DNA. He downloaded His compassion, His creativity, His warrior-worthy courage into your heart because He had a special job for you.

In the Old Testament, God told the prophet Jeremiah,

"Before I formed you in the womb I knew you, before you were born I set you apart; I appointed you as a prophet to the nations" (Jer 1:5). Even though the job of prophet was far from easy, God assured Jeremiah that He had created him specifically for that assignment. His life's work would hold both joy and great challenge, but God gave Jeremiah everything he needed to do the job he was chosen to do.

I believe that what God said to Jeremiah applies to you. I think He says to you, "Before I formed you in the womb, I knew you, before you were born, I set you apart; I chose you as…a teacher for my children.

"I chose you for the beautiful studious student who always gives the right answers…and the broken, disagreeable one who works your last nerve.

"I chose you for the student who comes in smiling every day…and the one who hasn't smiled all year.

"I chose you for the student who respects you and follows your lead…and the entitled one who expects to be the center of your universe.

"I chose you for the student who easily comprehends the demands of the curriculum…and the one who requires long hours of extra help from you.

"I chose you for the student whose parents make you feel like a hero…and the one whose parents make you feel like the problem."

Like Jeremiah, you didn't receive an easy assignment. In fact, if God hadn't downloaded all that strength, courage, creativity, and compassion into you, the job would be impossible. But you are chosen, and because you are chosen, you are equipped for the powerful, life-giving work of teaching. My prayer for you this week is that you will hear, above the noise of your own questions, God's voice whispering, *"You're the teacher I chose for the kids in your class."*

Dear Creator Father,

Thank You for creating me to teach and for putting in me exactly what I need to fulfill my calling. I know that You have chosen me as the teacher for every child You send me, but sometimes my own questions are louder than Your voice. Please speak Your peace to my spirit and remind me that You have set me apart for this divine work. In Jesus' name, Amen.

REFLECTIONS

1. Does the reminder from God that you are chosen to teach alter your perspective? How?

2. What are the heart-level questions about teaching that you may need to voice to God this week?

3. Read and meditate on Jeremiah 1:4–10 and record any insights God gives you about how His words to Jeremiah relate to you.

SCRIPTURES

"You did not choose me, but I chose you and appointed you so that you might go and bear fruit—fruit that will last—and so that whatever you ask in my name the Father will give you."
—John 15:16

"We have different gifts, according to the grace given to each of us. If your gift is prophesying, then prophesy in accordance with your faith; if it is serving, then serve; if it is teaching, then teach."

—Romans 12:6–7

"And God is able to bless you abundantly, so that in all things at all times, having all that you need, you will abound in every good work."

—2 Corinthians 9:8

For Such a Time as This
EQUIPPED TO TEACH IN DIFFICULT TIMES

• ————— • • • • ————— •

One of our best teachers popped her head in my office to say good morning, and I casually asked how she was doing. She tried to say, "Fine," but hesitated and drew in a deep breath. As we closed the door and sat down to talk, the tears she had been fighting broke loose. "I'm not sure I can do this anymore," she sobbed. "It's too much, and I'm too tired!"

Dedicated and passionate, this teacher gave everything she had every day, often sacrificing her own comfort, security, and sleep to make a difference in the lives of her students. And now her heart was broken by the demands of the job she loved, the strain of fatigue on her face as she worked to quiet her sobs.

Does your own heart echo that teacher's words? Do you feel that what is being asked of you is more than you can give? If you do, you are certainly not alone. Long hours, endless uncertainty, lack of respect, even threats to personal safety make it a tough time in history to be a teacher, even for those passionate about their calling.

But there is good news. When God chose us to teach, He also chose the exact time in history when our calling could have the greatest impact on the world. Yes, the times are challenging, but let me tell you one of my favorite stories in the Bible about a young woman who allowed God to use difficult times as the backdrop for one of His greatest miracles.

Esther was a Jewish orphan living in a foreign country where her family had been exiled years earlier. Raised by a godly uncle, she grew into a gracious, beautiful teenage girl who caught the eye of the king. Through a series of events only God could orchestrate, she became the queen of Persia.

While still barely out of her teens, she learned that her husband had been tricked into signing an order to annihilate the entire population of Jews in the kingdom. Those were her people, her relatives, her friends, and as queen, she was the only one with the power to save them. But there were great risks. Petitioning the king on their behalf would require her to reveal her Jewish heritage, a fact she'd kept hidden from the king. It would also mean defying the king's law that no one could enter his presence without being specifically called by him. Either act could mean instant death for Esther.

Esther's initial reluctance to intervene tells me that she felt what that sweet teacher in my office felt—that it was just too much. The environment was too hostile, the demands too great. But Esther made the decision to trust God, and the turning point for her came when she understood the truth of her uncle's words: *"And who knows but that you have come to your royal position for such a time as this?" (Est 4:14).*

For such a time as this…God chose Esther to be queen, and He chose her for a particular time because He knew what He had put in her heart. He knew that when times got tough, she would find her strength in Him and walk into her destiny with power. He knew that He had given her exactly what the times required and that she would come through for those depending on her courage. And that is what she did. After praying and fasting for three days, she stepped bravely into the king's inner court. God miraculously intervened, and the lives of her people were spared.

The "Esther" in my office did something similar. In that critical moment, she made a deliberate decision to trust that God had called her to her position for *such a time as this*. She stood, dried her eyes, and said, "Well, if it were easy, I guess anybody could do it." And she stepped bravely into the hallway to go back to her classroom. God miraculously intervened, strengthened her resolve to make a difference, and continues to touch the lives of students through her work.

These difficult teaching times have not caught God by surprise. In fact, He chose you *for* this time in history. You have a heart like Esther. You have her courage. People are depending on your courage, and God trusts you to come through. Yes, times are tough, and teaching is not easy, but you aren't just anybody! You can do this because God has chosen you for this work.

Now…

In this climate…

For such a time as this.

Dear Equipping Father,

I have always wanted to make a difference, but sometimes I wonder if I can overcome the demands of the times in which I teach. Remind me that You have chosen me, not only to teach but to teach in these exact times. Please don't let me forget that You are always with me, and it is by *Your* power that I can find courage to walk out my destiny so the lives of others can be touched by Your love. In Jesus' name, Amen.

Reflections

1. What is the "too much" in your life this week?

2. How does knowing that God has chosen you for this particular time in history change how you view the difficulties of your environment?

3. Spend time with God this week asking Him to give you the courage to walk with Him and trust Him to come through for you because He chose you for this time in history.

Scriptures

"David also said to Solomon his son, 'Be strong and courageous, and do the work. Do not be afraid or discouraged, for the LORD God, my God, is with you. He will not fail you or forsake you until all the work for the service of the temple of the LORD is finished.'"
—1 Chronicles 28:20

"Trust in the LORD with all your heart and lean not on your own understanding; in all your ways submit to him, and he will make your paths straight."
—Proverbs 3: 5–6

"Therefore, my dear brothers and sisters, stand firm. Let nothing move you. Always give yourselves fully to the work of the Lord, because you know that your labor in the Lord is not in vain."
—1 Corinthians 15:58

Buttercups
THE JOY OF PURPOSE

• ---- • • • • • ---- •

It is that time of the school year. The excitement of the new year has worn off, and the reality of what must be accomplished has set in. Long hours and little rest are taking their toll. You find your strength waning, your joy weakening, and your stress level growing. It is a familiar feeling for this time of the year, but every year it seems a little worse. If you are feeling a little low on strength and joy, I want to pray Nehemiah 8:10 over you this week. "The joy of the LORD is your strength!"

I'm asking God to renew your strength as He refills you with the joy of remembering your purpose for being a teacher. I want you, even if only for a short time, to block out the noise and meditate on the joy that was in your heart when teaching first became your passion. Hold on to that joy and let God strengthen you with power and purpose.

I found this excerpt in my journal and want to share it with you to remind you that you make a difference every day, and the difference you make reflects the beauty of a loving Creator who has called you to do something special.

I love buttercups. That's what we call them where I'm from. You may call them daffodils. I love the color,

I love the smell, and I especially love the sassiness of any flower with the nerve to bloom in early February in Middle Tennessee. Because I detest cold weather, I always welcome the breaks we get in the dead of winter when the temperature hovers in the 50s and 60s for a couple of weeks, and I anxiously watch to see if the stems of the buttercups are breaking through the ground. The excitement of seeing that beautiful spring green against the ugly brown of winter gives my soul a lift I can't even describe. Just when I think I can't take one more cold, dreary day, there they are, reminding me that spring will indeed come again this year. Oh, I know there will be more winter to endure, and I even worry each time I smell that first fragrant flower that it will get frozen by an almost certain blast of left-over winter. But that's another reason I love buttercups so much—I love the courage of any part of creation that dares to be obedient to a sovereign Creator coaxing it out of safety to be a soul refresher to those around it.

I want to be like the buttercups. I want to bloom in the middle of someone's winter and refresh their soul, even if it means allowing myself to be that vulnerable. I want to be someone's beautiful yellow during a time when they are expecting long months of winter brown. I want to be that unexpected fragrance that lifts someone's soul and reminds them that they can endure a little more winter because their heavenly Father will send spring right on time. I want to have the "sass" to defy the ugliness of the landscape and bloom like I own the meadow.

I pray that God reminds you this week that you are a buttercup. You are a difference maker. You change lives. You reflect the creative heart of God. You are God's hope in a world begging for someone to be vulnerable enough and brave enough to defy the ugliness of culture and bring beauty, direction, and wisdom into the lives of children. God sees the beauty of your heart, and He is honored by your obedience and courage. This week, turn your face to God and allow Him to strengthen you with the joy of knowing that His divine purpose is being accomplished through your work.

Dear Strength-Renewing Father,

I'm kind of tired right now. If I am completely honest, I'm wondering, as I do every year at this time, why I keep coming back to this job. Remind me again of my real purpose—to make a difference in the lives of those I teach—and strengthen me with the joy of knowing that You bring desperately needed beauty into the world through me. In Jesus' name, Amen.

REFLECTIONS

1. Remember the joy you felt when you first answered God's call to teach. What was it about teaching that stirred your sense of purpose?

2. What are ways you can increase your joy by bringing beauty into the lives of others this week?

3. Ask God to remind you of His purposes for you in teaching. Write them down and allow God to strengthen you this week by reminding you that His divine purpose is at work in you.

SCRIPTURES

"Go, eat your food with gladness, and drink your wine with a joyful heart, for God has already approved what you do."

—Ecclesiastes 9:7

"Many are the plans in a person's heart, but it is the LORD's purpose that prevails."

—Proverbs 19:21

"The LORD is my strength and my shield; my heart trusts in him, and he helps me. My heart leaps for joy, and with my song I praise Him. The LORD is the strength of his people, a fortress of salvation for his anointed one."

—Psalm 28:7–8

I'm So Happy!
EMBRACING THE GIFT OF TEACHING

• • • •

Retired grandparents took her in because one parent was in jail and the other locked in addiction. On their small pension, money was scarce, so when the glasses she desperately needed got broken in a playground accident, there was no money to repair them. Her vision was so dependent that, without glasses, learning was one more huge obstacle in this child's life.

The guidance counselor and I couldn't wait to surprise her with the new glasses a kind optometrist in town had made for her, so we called her to the office before the morning bell rang. Her eyes were full of questions as she peeked in my office door, but when she saw her shiny new pink frames, everything hard took a backseat to the joy. Jumping and clapping, her hazel eyes glowed with the appreciation of the words she kept repeating, "I'm so happy! I'm so happy! I'm so HAPPY!"

Her unbridled joy was contagious, and we couldn't help but share it as we watched through our tears as she skipped back to class. There were other things she could have focused on that morning. She could have reminded us that she needed so much more than just glasses. She could have recited all the problems the glasses wouldn't fix. She could have focused her mind on the difficulties still in her life, but she chose to focus instead on the joy of the gift.

I know that many days teaching feels like anything but a gift, but there really is no other job like it. In fact, I believe that deep down, most of us are crazy in love with this calling. It's just that our joy often gets obscured by the difficulties and demands. But this week, let's focus on what makes us happy about teaching. For the next few days, let's take our eyes off the problems and concentrate on the gift.

I chose three things to meditate on this week. From your own perspective, I'm sure you can come up with many more, but here are my three:

1. **Teachers reflect the creative heart of God.** (Genesis 1) God created the world and chose exactly what was needed to make everything flow. He created order and precision. He created procedures and rhythms so that the world could function productively. He filled the world with light and life. Doesn't He allow us to do that every year? Aren't we reflecting God's own creative heart when we put order and rhythm into our classroom world so children can learn and grow? Aren't we mirroring our Creator as we orchestrate function out of chaos? Doesn't He allow us to join hands with Him in sustaining life as we plant seeds of knowledge and wisdom into future generations? What a gift!

2. **Teachers share the ministry of Jesus.** In His life on Earth, Jesus was a teacher. John 13:13 says, *"You call me 'Teacher' and 'Lord' and rightly so, for that is what I am."* It was who He was, and it is who we are. When we teach with compassion or empower our students to be

all they can be, we are joining in the work of the Master Teacher. When we model and teach kindness and grace and forgiveness, we are allowing the teaching heart of Jesus to flow through us. When we take the time to know our kids and to meet them at their point of need, we are continuing the work of Jesus. When we realize that God sent us to Earth with a job to do, and when we dedicate our efforts to His glory, we share the ministry of our Lord. What a gift!

3. **Teachers spend their days in the presence of God.** In Mark 9:36–37, Jesus took a little child and had him stand among the disciples. Then He took the child in His arms and said, *"Whoever welcomes one of these little children in my name welcomes me; and whoever welcomes me…welcomes the one who sent me."* Think about what Jesus is saying. Let it sink in that He loves children so much that He occupies the space where they are welcomed. Every day when we welcome our students, God is joining us. When we help our students recognize their value, when we love the ones who are hard to love, when we create a classroom culture where all children find dignity and belonging, we are sharing our classroom space with Almighty God. What a gift!

I know you have lesson plans to write this week. I know that parent conference you have scheduled this week may be difficult. I know you may have a child in your class who is driving you crazy. I know how hard this job is. But this week, let's remember what a gift it is. Let's focus on the unique, the amazing, the anointed. Let's remember what we get to do that nobody else gets to do. In the middle of this crazy week, let's choose to focus on the joy of the gift.

Dear Gift-Giving Father,

I'm in awe that You would choose me to receive this amazing gift of being called Teacher. Thank You for placing Your creative, compassionate heart in me and for placing me where I can reflect that to Your precious children. You understand that there are many hard things about what I do, but please help me remember to accept Your gift with appreciation because You don't let just anybody do this job. In Jesus' name, Amen.

REFLECTIONS

1. Name one way you reflected the creative heart of God this week.

2. Share a time from this week when joining the compassionate work of Jesus made you happy.

3. How will you welcome the presence of God into your classroom this week by welcoming His children?

SCRIPTURES

"For the LORD God is a sun and shield, the LORD bestows favor and honor; no good thing does he withhold from those whose walk is blameless."

—Psalm 84:11

"A generous person will prosper; whoever refreshes others will be refreshed."

—Proverbs 11:25

"Every good and every perfect gift is from above, coming down from the Father of the heavenly lights, who does not change like shifting shadows."

—James 1:17

Remembering the Why
OUR LOVE FOR SERVING

•———— • • • • ————•

"He who has a why to live can bear almost any how."
—Friedrich Nietzsche

Our staff was exhausted. We had processed too much new information since school began in August and fought our way through new leadership, new instructional mandates, and new intervention procedures. By the time Christmas vacation came, we had nothing left. Our brains were overloaded, our hearts were undernourished, and our spirits were, frankly, uninspired.

As our leadership team sat to plan the new material we were to present on the teachers' first day back from vacation, we knew the emotional condition of our colleagues. "Let's just make blankets," one of the team members said. He had read an article about the homeless families in our community and how they were suffering from our unusually cold Tennessee winter. We looked at him like he had lost his mind. "We need to remember why we do this job," he insisted. None of us got the connection, but if it meant we could put off unpacking new state standards for a couple of hours, we would try anything.

We bought six fleece blanket kits and had them ready when teachers came in the library that morning. Everyone was excited to try something new, and we all felt good about spending our time to help others, but no one anticipated the profound impact that activity would have on our entire staff.

I believe the Holy Spirit entered our library as we gathered on the floor around our two raw pieces of fleece, cutting strips and tying the two pieces together to make heavy cozy blankets. Energy and excitement filled the room as loving hands worked to make gifts for perfect strangers. Smiles flashed and happy tears flowed as teams stood together for pictures with their finished products, and surprising joy shone on faces that only an hour before were creased with dread or resignation. Fresh purpose flowed through our conversations as our library became sacred ground and God stripped away all our distractions to remind us why we love this job.

Our teammate had been right. The connection finally hit us. We loved teaching because we loved serving. We loved serving because we loved enriching the lives of those around us. In fact, it seemed we found our greatest joy when we saw a clear connection between our efforts and their impact on those we served.

There is a reason serving others inspires us. 1 Peter 4:10 tells us: *"Each of you should use whatever gift you have received to serve others, as faithful stewards of God's grace in its various forms."*

We have been given a gift from God to teach and the primary purpose of that gift is to allow God's grace to flow through us as we serve others. That is why we were so inspired by making blankets. When we made the connection between our gift and how it would improve the lives of the families in our community, we felt the joy of God's grace flowing through us and it filled us with purpose and inspiration.

Why don't we feel that same inspiration every day in our classrooms? Why did it take an activity like making blankets to remind us of how much we love serving? Maybe it's because our brains, hearts, and spirits operate on overload most of the time, and it's hard to see what we do every day as service. The joy of serving often gets concealed behind the staggering requirements of this job.

But through our blanket-making activity, God reminded our staff that day that our love for teaching is rooted in our love for serving. It changed the way we looked at our everyday work and encouraged us to uncover all the ways we use the gifts we have received to serve others. He wants you to feel what we felt. He wants you to feel inspired instead of exhausted. He wants you to have fresh energy and purpose by remembering why you teach.

So, I am offering a challenge. This week, perform a simple act of service for someone. By yourself or with your team or even as a staff, just for the reminder of what it feels like when you administer God's grace through service. Then, read 1 Peter 4:10 every day and ask God to show you how your gift of teaching is being used to serve others. Finally, take just one difficult part of your teaching assignment and break it down to find the potential for service hidden behind the demand. Try to be intentional this week in remembering that using your gift to serve others for God is why you do this job.

Dear Grace-Administering Father,

Thank You for trusting me with precious gifts from You. Thank You for trusting me with the people You have put in my path to serve. Help me remember that it is a gift to serve others and that You are using me to administer Your grace to those I serve. Lord, many times my joy of serving gets hidden behind paperwork and meetings and exhaustion from the demands of teaching. This week, please make me aware of how everything I do in my job has the potential for service. Fill me with the fresh inspiration of remembering that I love teaching because You have placed the love for serving in my heart. In Jesus' name, Amen.

REFLECTIONS

1. What was your deliberate act of service? Share how you felt God's grace flow through you.

2. Spend time with God and ask Him to reveal hidden ways He has embedded service into all the components of your job. Journal those revelations.

3. How did you receive fresh inspiration from remembering that you teach because God has gifted you to serve?

SCRIPTURES

"The greatest among you will be your servant. For those who exalt themselves will be humbled, and those who humble themselves will be exalted."
—Matthew 23:11–12

"For even the Son of Man did not come to be served, but to serve, and to give his life as a ransom for many."
—Mark 10:45

"Give, and it will be given to you. A good measure, pressed down, shaken together and running over, will be poured into your lap. For with the measure you use, it will be measured to you."

—Luke 6:38

Part Two
Restoring Peace and Joy

God Is the Source

Thankfulness
THE SECRET TO A HEART OF PEACE

• • • •

Donnie was one of those students you never forget. He was smart, generous and kind, and his spirit was quiet and gentle. And those eyes! Those huge brown eyes were warm and tender and there was a peace in them that I didn't understand.

Donnie's life was tough. He worked hard but struggled to keep up with our second-grade work because he missed so much school. Both parents were alcoholics, so devastated by the disease that they were barely able to retain custody of their two children. Donnie, at seven, was caregiver to his parents, his five-year-old sister, and himself. If he didn't wake up, get his sister up, get them both fed, dressed, and at the bus stop on time, they missed school. And they missed school a lot.

But Donnie was present on the day in mid-November when we studied the first Thanksgiving. Our class discussed ways each family celebrated the holiday and what it meant to be thankful. Then, for fun, we traced our hands to make the shape of a turkey, and I asked them to write something on each feather that made them thankful.

That assignment was harder for my students than I thought it would be. They struggled to think of four things they were thankful for. But I noticed that Donnie started writing immediately and by the time I walked across the classroom to his desk, his turkey feathers were filled. *Family, School, Jesus, Love.* He ran out of feathers before he ran out of thankfulness, so he stuck the word *Sister* on his turkey's head.

The child whose life had dealt him the toughest hand was the quickest to express his gratitude. And he was thankful for things the rest of us complained about, ignored, or took for granted. As I stood speechless beside his desk, he looked up at me and smiled. "Here," he said, handing me his paper, "you can keep this."

What Donnie handed me that day was much more than a child's drawing; it was a treasure map. He offered me a way to find the peace I saw in his wise eyes. I'm pretty sure he couldn't recite 1 Thessalonians 5:18, but his life was an example of it: *"Be joyful always, pray continually, give thanks in all circumstances, for this is God's will for you in Christ Jesus."*

Donnie didn't discount the difficulty of his situation. He understood very well that he was being asked to carry a heavier load than most. I just think he knew the secret to living a life in God's will even in the middle of struggle, and his secret was thankfulness. He opened his eyes to see beyond his circumstances to the goodness of God who knows how to give "good and perfect gifts." Acknowledging those gifts increased his trust, and his trust in the goodness of God was the foundation for his peace.

Giving thanks in all circumstances is God's will for us because He knows it ultimately is the key to our peace. Maybe this week when we are tempted to let the difficulties of teaching make us miserable, we can think about Donnie's "treasure map." When we want to complain about the unfair, the unmanageable, the unpleasant, we can just stop and take a breath and fill the feathers of our own turkey. We can be deliberate about acknowledging what God has done and what He is doing, and we can thank Him.

As we focus on being thankful, our trust in God's goodness will grow, and when our trust expands, we experience God's peace, which is greater than anything we can understand (Phil 4:7).

Dear Peace-Giving Father,

I get it! I understand that being thankful is Your will for me because You want me to have peace in my heart. Thank You for what You have done, what You are doing, and what You will do because You love me and want to give me good and perfect gifts. Help me to see beyond my circumstances and open my eyes to Your gifts every day. Help me to be deliberate about thanking You. In Jesus' name, Amen.

REFLECTIONS

1. Does "giving thanks in all circumstances" come naturally for you? Why or why not?

2. How do you choose to be deliberate this week about noticing God's gifts and thanking Him for them?

3. Notice any ways that making the choice to be thankful brings you more peace.

SCRIPTURES

"Enter his gates with thanksgiving and his courts with praise; give thanks to him and praise his name. For the LORD is good and his love endures forever, his faithfulness continues through all generations."

—Psalm 100:4–5

"O LORD, you are my God: I will exalt you and praise your name, for in perfect faithfulness, you have done marvelous things, things planned long ago."

—Isaiah 25:1

"Let the peace of Christ rule in your hearts, since as members of one body you were called to peace. And be thankful…And whatever you do, whether in word or deed, do it all in the name of the Lord Jesus, giving thanks to God the Father through him."

—Colossians 3:15, 17

Sacrifice of Praise
I DON'T NEED ATTITUDE FROM YOU

• • • •

It was 8:45 a.m. and already an argument in the car-rider line had cars backed up so far, they blocked the busy highway in front of our school. More teachers were out with the flu than we had substitutes available. One of the bathrooms had backed up again, and the hallway smelled like a sewer. Then the call came over my radio, "Mrs. Tidwell, could you please come to the office?"

I heard the parent's shouts before I could open the security doors from the hallway. *Really?* I thought. *Now?* I was in no mood for more problems, but this woman's anger escalated with each attempt by our receptionist to respond to her shouted demands. I stepped in, and in what I thought was my most diplomatic voice, I explained—between the parent's outbursts—that being tardy twenty-four times in one school year was neither good for her child nor respectful for the teacher and other students in the class.

Maybe my face exposed my exasperated heart or maybe my words were spoken before I could temper my own frustration; I don't know. I do know that she put her finger in my face, waved it back and forth in that Z pattern middle-school girls use to let you know they mean business, and yelled, "I don't need this place. I don't need these people telling me what to do. And I don't need *attitude* from *you!*"

We all stood there, mouths gaping and eyes wide, as we watched her storm out the door. Somebody from the office walked the kids to class and got them settled (for the twenty-fourth time), and I went to my office to catch my breath before the data meeting, scheduled just fifteen minutes later. As I opened my planner to scan the appointments for the day, my eyes landed on the daily Scripture at the top of the page. "Through Jesus, therefore, let us continually offer to God a sacrifice of praise—the fruit of lips that openly profess his name" (Heb 13:15).

I laughed out loud. Praising God was the last thing I wanted to do. I wanted to scream with frustration. I wanted to sit and number my offenses and complain about the impossibility of a job that makes me want to cry before nine a.m.

But that's not where God wanted me that morning, so He kept whispering, "Sacrifice of praise" until I opened the Bible in my top drawer and found the Psalms. Scanning the pages for verses I had underlined or words I had written in the margins, I began to speak the promises of God out loud, right there in my office.

He is a shield around me (3:3).
Deliverance comes from Him (3:8).
He hears when I call to Him (4:3).
He blesses me and surrounds me with favor (5:12).
He is a refuge, a place of safety in troubled times. He has never ignored those who seek Him (9:9–10).
He is my strength (18:1).
He turns crying into dancing and covers me with joy (30:11–12).

Praise turned my morning around. Remembering God's promises through speaking His word and truth into my circumstances changed my outlook. The situation hadn't changed, but what had seemed impossible only minutes before could now be laid at His feet with confidence.

My spoken praise reminded me of God's love for me and His power over anything I faced. Where the enemy had me looking at problems, praise lifted my eyes to the love and power of a mighty God. I could even acknowledge that maybe, just maybe, God used that mama's angry words about my attitude as a teachable moment to make me more like Him.

I know you have mornings like this one. Probably more than you can count. Mornings when you feel more like crying than praising. Mornings when the unfairness of this job takes center stage in your heart and one problem after another overwhelms the possibilities you had envisioned for your day. Mornings when someone's angry choices threaten your mood and disrupt your teaching.

Friends, the enemy of our soul understands that mood. He knows when things aren't going our way, when we feel discouraged and bitter, and he knows how to exploit our challenges to keep us stuck in a sour, unproductive place. He wants our focus on the impossibility of this job.

But God wants us back in the fight. He has given us this teaching assignment that only we can do, and He knows that when the enemy entices us to focus on our limitations, praise turns our focus back to the limitless power of God.

This week let's be deliberate about praising God. On those days when the enemy has you looking down, my prayer is that you will offer your sacrifice of praise. Let your lips confess His name and His good works. Allow God to lift your eyes to Him and fill you with the truth of His love for you.

It may feel like a sacrifice at first to let go of your dark mood, but the new attitude and new hope and strength to live out your calling will soon feel much more like victory than sacrifice.

Dear Praiseworthy Father,

I need to confess to You that this is a day when praising You is not what comes naturally. Honestly, I feel more like wallowing in that place where my focus is on everything that is wrong. Sometimes, that is a comfortable place. But that doesn't honor You, and it doesn't accomplish Your purpose. Remind me to look up and to focus on who *You* are. Form words of praise on my lips as I look to You for a new attitude of victory. In Jesus' name, Amen.

REFLECTIONS

1. Identify situations at school that tend to derail your day and keep you stuck in a dark mood of discouragement.

2. As you reflect on what "sacrifice of praise" means to you, what do you sense God asking you to do?

3. Make your own praise list or use the Psalm verses I shared to speak God's truth over your challenges this week. What do you notice?

SCRIPTURES

"My mouth is filled with your praise, declaring your splendor all day long."
—Psalm 71:8

"I will proclaim the name of the LORD. Oh, praise the greatness of our God! He is the Rock, his works are perfect, and all his ways are just. A faithful God who does no wrong, upright and just is he."

—Deuteronomy 32: 3–4

"If anyone speaks, they should do so as one who speaks the very words of God. If anyone serves, they should do so with the strength God provides, so that in all things God may be praised through Jesus Christ."

—1 Peter 4:11

Katherine's Boo-Boo
CAPTIVATING GOD'S HEART WITH OUR TRUST

· · · ·

On an unusually warm spring afternoon, the kids were enjoying extra time on the playground when Katherine rushed up to me and held out her hand. "Look! I got a boo-boo!" I could see only a tiny scratch, so I kissed it and reassured her that she was okay. A look of peace settled in her deep blue eyes as they connected with mine. She smiled and immediately went back to the joy of playing with her friends.

In that blink of time, God gave me a glimpse into His heart. He drew my full attention to how quickly Katherine's joy was restored because she trusted me and brought her pain immediately to me. Instead of fretting over her injury, she allowed her trust in my reassurance to fill her with peace. I would have moved mountains for Katherine in that moment, not because her injury required it, but because the intimacy of her trust captivated my heart.

What happened that day changed my perspective on how I trust God. For the most part, I had learned to trust God with my epic hurts. I have lived through times of suffering when I had no choice but to hold onto Him with everything in me. Through this young child, though, I realized God was also inviting me to trust Him with the small injuries, the "scratches," those times when my feelings got hurt by thoughtless words, times I felt excluded, when my efforts went unnoticed or unappreciated, times I craved praise and acceptance but got stung by rejection, times when one more job got added to my plate…the list could go on and on. That day, I sensed His whisper that more joy and peace were available to me if I trusted Him like Katherine trusted me.

Honestly, running to God with my everyday hurts is not my first thought. I am much more likely to nurse little injuries like they are giant wounds. I tend to throw my peace away by rehashing tiny offenses in my mind or crafting prideful ways to redeem my ego. Sometimes, I even carelessly steal the joy and peace of others by retelling my version of a small wound, giving it energy to become something much bigger than it needs to be. I can be that person who turns tiny, everyday scratches into emergency-sized injuries that obscure my peace for days.

But I want something different. I want to trust Him more intimately. I want to feel the peace of His reassurance as I face the everyday scratches of life. I want my joy restored quickly so I spend less time fretting and more time living. I want that for you, too, so this week let's claim God's promise in Romans 15:13: "May the God of hope fill you with all joy and peace as you trust in him, so that you may overflow with hope by the power of the Holy Spirit."

Isn't that a beautiful promise? Not only does God fill us with joy and peace in exchange for our trust in Him, He fills us so full that those around us are gloriously touched by the hope ignited in our hearts through our trust in Him.

This week I will do things a little differently, and I invite you to join me in claiming this promise of peace, joy, and hope. Let's take God at His word. Let's run straight to Him with our needs, stretch out our hand, and give our scratches to Him. Let's listen for His voice of reassurance and trust Him when He says we're okay. Let's allow Him to quickly restore our joy so that what overflows from us reflects His hope to those around us. Let's allow God to move mountains for us, not because the size of our injury requires it, but because His heart is captivated by the intimacy of our trust.

Dear Trustworthy Father,

I confess to You that I have not been good about trusting You with everyday hurts. Usually, instead of bringing them immediately to You, I hold onto them and sometimes I waste a lot of time and energy making them bigger than they really are. But I know that is not what You want for me. Help me to trust You with everyday battles so that You can fill me with joy and peace. I want Your hope to overflow from me to everyone around me this week. In Jesus' name, Amen.

REFLECTIONS

1. As you go through this week, what do you notice about your tendencies to hold onto hurt instead of taking it immediately to God?

2. Are you noticing areas where you could have more peace and joy through trusting God?

3. Pay attention to specific times this week when you take your scratches straight to God. How was God able to fill you so that your hope could overflow to someone else?

SCRIPTURES

"Many are the woes of the wicked, but the LORD's unfailing love surrounds the one who trusts in him."

—Psalm 32:10

"How gracious he will be when you cry for help! As soon as he hears, he will answer you."

—Isaiah 30:19

"Let us then approach God's throne of grace with confidence, so that we may receive mercy and find grace to help us in our time of need."

—Hebrews 4:16

What Happened to Your Joy?
MY JOY JOURNEY

* * * *

"To miss the joy is to miss everything."
—Robert Louis Stevenson

A retired teacher friend invited me to lunch on a particularly tough day. "How is school?" she asked, and I'm certain it took only moments for her to wish she hadn't asked. Describing the frustrations and challenges from the months since she had been gone, my response was full of despair and envy. Her voice was filled with compassion and her eyes with tenderness, but her next question was a bombshell. "What happened to all of your joy?"

I didn't know the answer. I guess I hadn't even realized I had become so joyless. I didn't know how I had reached that place. I wanted to reflect God's joy in my work, but my joy was buried under the daily demands of my job. Something had to change. And it would start with me rediscovering my joy for teaching. My remedy…a Joy Journey.

For an entire year, I read and meditated on Scriptures about joy and tried to allow the truths of those Scriptures to sink deep into my spirit. I kept a Joy Journal and at the end of each day, I journaled the things that had brought me joy. What I learned was life-changing.

What about you? If you were to talk to my friend in the

teachers' lounge this week, would she ask you the same question? Have you lost your joy? Do you feel a little desperate to have it back in your life? If that describes you, maybe you can find encouragement this week in the lessons I learned on my Joy Journey.

1. Joy is available to me any time, no matter the circumstance. People pass in and out of my life, situations change, things that I hold dear sometimes disappear. But joy is always available to me if I remain close to Jesus. He is the source of my joy. He is my friend when I am lonely, my confidante when I feel abandoned, my healer when my wounds are deep, my surprise-giver when I least expect a miracle, my cleanser when a spiritual bath is in order. He opens the door to my Father's love, and as long as I stick with Him—in His Word, in prayer, and in following His teachings—the joy remains available.

2. Joy is a verb. (Okay, for you English teachers, I know not really.) My point is that joy requires action. It requires deliberate choice. I must get rid of old patterns and find new ways to grow in order to make room for the joy I seek. My bitterness, anger, and hurtful intentions are joy blockers. They must go. I must make the deliberate choice, moment by moment, to reject them.

3. An ungrateful heart blocks joy. I must stop comparing my life to others'. Comparison leads to unrealistic expectations, and unrealistic expectations lead to an ungrateful heart. Gratitude for my own special place in God's heart is the beginning of joy for me. Knowing that He has a plan that is suited just for me makes me look up to Him for His guidance. Trusting that He is good and that, somehow,

He will work everything that happens to me for good, changes my perspective. I can be grateful, even in my difficult times, because I see His love at work, testing and purifying and removing those things that block my joy.

4. Acknowledgment of gifts that I would ordinarily call "little" makes me more appreciative of the many moments of joy God showers on me. As I notice and write down the daily things that bring joy into my life, I learn that goals are necessary, and dreams are life-giving, but it is the everyday joy moments that truly define a life well lived. Tuning my heart to acknowledge those moments means I no longer have to search for joy. I find it over and over in the tiny moments of my life.

5. Words hold joy potential, but I waste a lot of joy on the words I choose. When I choose complaining, judging, and gossiping, it's because I want them to make me feel more powerful. But they have the opposite effect. They drain my joy. When I deliberately choose words that build others up, give grace, and reflect my faith in God's goodness, my heart is lighter and life holds more hope. The power of life and death is truly in the tongue. It holds the power to affect others and the power to increase or diminish my own joy.

6. Forgiveness releases joy. Unforgiveness blocks joy. It's so simple, yet so difficult. Forgiveness doesn't necessarily equal a renewal of trust. Forgiveness doesn't necessarily equal a repair of the relationship, but I forgive because I have been forgiven, and it frees my soul to experience joy again.

7. "Growth, not perfection" is a mantra of joy. I find spiritu-

al rest in knowing God will finish what He started in me. I don't have to be perfect. I can't be perfect. I don't even want to be perfect. I just want to grow every day in being who He created me to be.

Dear Joy-Giving Father,

I know it is important to You that I experience Your joy and reflect it to those around me. I confess, I am having a hard time being joyful right now. I have spent more time noticing things that are hard and less time being aware of the many joy-filled moments You give. Help me to stay in Your presence where joy abides. Give me the desire and the discipline to get rid of anything that needs to go so I can make room for more joy. Renew my gratitude for all You do for me and refresh my work with the strength of Your joy. In Jesus' name, Amen.

REFLECTIONS

1. How does joy or a lack of joy impact the effectiveness of your teaching?

2. Is there anything blocking your joy? Anything you need to get rid of to make room for joy?

3. Try keeping a Joy Journal for a week. At the end of each day, write down everything that brought you joy that day. At the end of the week, look back at what you wrote and ask God to show you any lessons you learned about joy.

SCRIPTURES

"Yet I will rejoice in the LORD, I will be joyful in God my Savior."

—Habakkuk 3:18

"When anxiety was great within me, your consolation brought me joy."

—Psalm 94:19

"You have made known to me the paths of life; you will fill me with joy in your presence."

—Acts 2:28

Beyond What We Can See
SUPERNATURAL HELP

* * * *

We all knew her well. Mrs. P. had delivered and picked up her grandsons almost every day for the past four years. A devoted grandmother and retired teacher, she was one of our favorites. Her last year had been tough, though. Diagnosed with cancer, she had suffered through two surgeries and needed another to repair damage to her back caused by the cancer treatments.

I saw her from my office window walking up the sidewalk to the front entrance of our school and knew she was checking the boys out to meet their mom for a dentist appointment. Tears of pain streaked her face as she struggled to walk the distance between her car and our front door. Jumping up from my desk, I called out that Mrs. P. needed help, but before I could finish the sentence, the entire front office staff jumped into action. We grabbed a rolling chair, sprinted out the door and halfway down the sidewalk to meet her, caught her in the chair, and rolled her the rest of the way to the office.

Tears of gratitude overran her tears of pain. "Well, I didn't see that coming," she said. "How'd you even know I needed help?"

She didn't know I had been watching her from my window. She couldn't see us scrambling to get out the door with the chair. And, because of what she couldn't see, she thought that her struggle was invisible. She thought that her painful walk was something she had to do alone.

Sometimes teaching can feel like that. Like no one notices or stands with us in our struggles. Sometimes, the next step seems impossible because we think we're alone. But help is there, even when we can't see it, and 2 Kings 6 is a beautiful illustration of that help.

Elisha, God's prophet to Israel, infuriated an enemy king by supernaturally foiling all his plans to attack Israel. Determined to capture and kill the pesky prophet, the king sent an army of horses and chariots during the night to surround the city where Elisha stayed. When Elisha's servant went outside the next morning, he saw the surrounding army ready to advance on the two of them.

Can you identify with the servant's response? "Oh no, my lord! What shall we do?" (2 Kings 6:15). Can you hear the desperation in his voice? Can you imagine how isolated he must have felt, knowing that only the two of them faced that vast army? Can you identify with his panic, thinking God had forgotten them?

But Elisha had a different perspective. He knew His God was watching. He knew His God wouldn't fail him. He knew His God was mighty and had more resources than their human eyes could see. And he knew His God would send help right on time. There was no panic in his voice when he prayed, "Open his eyes, LORD, so that he may see" (2 Kings 6:17).

The Lord opened the servant's eyes, and he saw horses and chariots of fire all around them. They were surrounded by the supernatural forces of God, and the king's army was no match for God's army. Heavenly warriors, standing ready beyond what human eyes could see, helped Elisha and his servant capture the entire enemy army. God had been there all along, watching and preparing His heavenly resources for battle.

God is there for you too. He sees you grading those papers after your own kids are in bed. He watches you sit in those endless meetings when you have so much to do. He sees your impossible schedule. Behind your classroom door when it seems no one cares how hard you work, God cares. He knows the work you do. He knows what terrifies you and what threatens to overcome your heart. He knows the battles you face. He knows what you need. And He stands ready with limitless resources to send for your victory.

This week, let's ask God to open our eyes so we can see how He walks with us on this journey. Let's look for His presence and provision, which are all around us. Let's remind ourselves that the tea left on our desk by a friend was really a gift from God. That the unexpected hug from a child was God sending encouragement. That the canceled meeting was God giving us more time. That the extra courage or compassion coming out of nowhere during a parent meeting was God's answer to prayer. That the homemade guacamole and chips a parent left in the lounge...well, that was just God showing off for us because He knows we like to eat.

Friends, we are not invisible, and we don't walk this journey alone. So when your next step seems impossible, trust in what you can't see. God is with you, and help is on the way.

Dear Army-Sending Father,

I want to take a moment to thank You for always being there for me. Even when I can't see You, I know You are with me. But sometimes, I need to be reminded of Your presence. I need to be reminded that You fight battles for me. I need to be reminded that You know what I need when I need it, and that You meet me where I am with Your unlimited resources. Open my eyes this week to see that I am never alone and never without everything I need. In Jesus' name, Amen.

REFLECTIONS

1. Does Elisha's story change your perspective about feeling alone or invisible in your work?

2. How do you need God to come through for you this week?

3. After praying for God to open your eyes, were you able to see ways He supernaturally intervened in your struggle this week? Were you surprised by anything you noticed?

SCRIPTURES

"For the LORD your God is the one who goes with you to fight for you against your enemies to give you victory."
—Deuteronomy 20:4

"I lift up my eyes to the mountains—where does my help come from? My help comes from the LORD, the Maker of heaven and earth."
—Psalm 121:1–2

"So we fix our eyes not on what is seen, but on what is unseen, since what is seen is temporary, but what is unseen is eternal."

  —2 Corinthians 4:18

Part Three:

DECLARING VICTORY

TRUSTING GOD'S POWER IN DIFFICULT TIMES

Manna
GOD'S ANSWER WHEN WE FEEL OVERWHELMED

• • • •

1978…One room, one teacher, thirteen students, seven grade levels.

That was my life the year I taught country school in central South Dakota. Located twenty miles from the nearest town, my school served six farm families spread out over thousands of acres of prairie land. Like spokes on a wagon wheel, seven country schools surrounded the one school in town, but mine was the only school with at least one child in every grade level K–6. My daily schedule included seven reading groups, seven math groups, and seven lessons of spelling, English, science, and social studies.

Because I was the only adult, duty-free time didn't exist. In addition to academics, I functioned as the school nurse, art teacher, P.E. teacher, recess supervisor, and lunch lady. Since there was no time in the daily schedule for planning, every Friday, I piled teacher's manuals in the back seat of my Ford Grenada and spent the entire weekend writing lesson plans, which required approval by the town principal before school each Monday morning.

It was exhausting; it felt impossible; and I was completely overwhelmed. I know you understand what I'm describing. In fact, I can visualize your head nodding as you think about your own assignment. I feel your heart sighing from the weight of your impossible tasks and limited resources. I understand the depth of spiritual exhaustion you can feel when you just can't get caught up.

If overwhelmed is how you are feeling right now, the story in Exodus 16 may encourage you and remind you of how loving and faithful God is, especially in those times when the demands of our circumstances outweigh our obvious resources. The children of Israel were wandering in the desert.

Only a few months earlier, they had been slaves, working under horrific conditions. Their escape from Egypt was miraculous, but terrifying. Their new desert living conditions were foreign and confusing. Their food supply had run out and starvation was a real possibility. Those chosen children were reeling from the trauma of slavery, exhausted from the physical demands of their journey, unsure of how to navigate a desert, and terrified of dying from hunger. "Overwhelmed" may be a gross understatement!

The children of Israel didn't always respond to challenges in ways that honored God, and that gives me hope. Most of the time I don't handle tough times well, either. My tendencies are to panic and complain like they did. But I'm so thankful that our human shortcomings don't define the love of our God. When Moses brought the people's needs to God, the divine response was immediate and miraculous. "I'm going to rain down bread from heaven for you" (Ex 16:4). And, just like that, God took care of their needs. He didn't remove them from the difficult situation because He had a purpose for their time in the desert, but every morning for the next forty years, fresh, hunger-stopping manna appeared right on time.

Let's just take a deep breath and inhale the truth from that

Scripture. Just for a moment, hear God telling us that He knows our situation. That when He chooses us for seemingly impossible tasks, He never leaves us to accomplish them with our own limited human capabilities.

I want to tell you the rest of my country school story because it is my own personal application of Exodus 16, and maybe you will find encouragement in what God did for me. Amid an impossible assignment, God surrounded me with divine, miraculous manna daily. I didn't always focus on it, and when I didn't, I was miserable. But when I looked for it, God's love and provision were there, giving me exactly what I needed. My heart smiles all these years later when I think about the joy of that unique assignment. I'm not sure which memory is my favorite…

- watching students across multiple grade levels help and learn from each other

- the deep connections made sharing life around our lunch table

- piling all thirteen students in the back of a family's pickup to sled *all afternoon* after a big snow

- how hard I laughed the day one of my fifth graders jumped up in the middle of class to grab a baseball bat and take out a mouse

- my gratitude for the kindness of the dad who drove me to town in his four-wheel-drive truck when the ice storm hit

- how we all celebrated the day we got the snake out of the basement

Manna was all around me when I took my focus off the

difficulty of my assignment and opened my eyes to God's loving provision for me. He didn't take me out of my tough situation because He had purpose for it; He was laying a foundation for success that couldn't have happened any other way.

God is providing manna for you too. It's all around you, and it is exactly what you need every day. My prayer for you this week is that God will open your eyes to His manna for you, and that you will revel in the joy of His supernatural provision raining down on you from heaven right now and for as long as you need it.

Dear Manna-Providing Father,

Things are a little overwhelming for me right now. I'm not sure I'm up to the task You have given me. It feels impossible. Please remind me of Your love for me. Remind me of the on-time, life-sustaining manna you gave the children of Israel when they were ready to give up. Open my eyes to see how You are providing exactly what I need and let the depth of Your love for me be the only thing that overwhelms me this week. In Jesus' name, Amen.

REFLECTIONS

1. What is making you feel overwhelmed?

2. What are some ways you can adjust your focus so you can be aware of the manna God is providing?

3. How can you be part of God's manna for someone else who is feeling overwhelmed this week?

SCRIPTURES

"I am the LORD your God, who brought you up out of Egypt. Open wide your mouth and I will fill it."

—Psalms 81:10

"The LORD your God among you is powerful—he will save and he will take joyful delight in you. In his love he will renew you with his love; he will celebrate with singing because of you."

—Zephaniah 3:17, ISV

"And my God will supply every need of yours according to His riches in glory in Christ Jesus."

—Philippians 4:19

Stand Up!
GOD'S PLAN FOR OVERCOMING DEFEAT

• • • •

I was twenty-five years old and a three-year teaching veteran when defeat nearly derailed my career. I knew my country school assignment on the South Dakota prairie would be tough, but teaching students in seven grade levels sounded interesting. I had three years under my belt, one in a Tennessee classroom and two on a South Dakota Sioux Reservation. I thought I could handle the challenge, but by late September I realized I was in way over my head.

Asking for help was the only solution I could envision, so I went to my town principal to ask for a teaching assistant. Without the funds or the authority to add a position, he suggested that I present my request to the local school board.

Summoning my courage, I prepared a presentation and asked for a meeting with the four-member school board made up of weathered farmers each old enough to be my grandfather. I knew it wasn't going well when they sat without motion or expression during my presentation, but I was not prepared for the only question they would ask me. "Young lady, how long did you say you have been teaching?" That was their response to my request for help. They chalked up my need to my inexperience and emphatically and unanimously turned down my request.

My defeat was resounding and humiliating. I spent that night and many more sprawled across my bed sobbing and vowing to quit and move back to Tennessee. I was discouraged and disoriented, looking for somewhere to hide, someone to blame, and permission from God to give up.

Have you ever experienced a time when you put your heart on the line and had it handed back to you in defeat? Maybe you are walking through painful discouragement right now. If you are, my heart hurts for you, but I know God has a victory waiting. The Bible is full of stories of folks like you and me who walked through times of defeat. My favorite is Joshua's, when he lost a battle he expected to win. I get so much encouragement from his story because I can relate to his reaction.

Joshua led the people of Israel after Moses died. He was smart and courageous, and he had seen God come through in battle time after time. Because of a couple of critical mistakes, he suffered a humiliating defeat at the hands of a small army. Because Joshua was accustomed to winning battles, the defeat temporarily paralyzed him. He lay on the ground in dismay, questioning God's wisdom, protection, and promise.

God's response to Joshua may seem a little blunt, but it was exactly what he needed to hear. It is what I needed to hear as I lay across my bed, and it is most likely what you need to hear if you are experiencing the discouragement of defeat. You can read Joshua 7–8 to get God's entire message to Joshua, but let me give you the three main points that captured my attention:

1. **Stand up! What are you doing down on your face?**

   God wasn't mad at Joshua for pouring out his heart. God's

shoulders are always broad enough to bear our honest emotions. He just knew that living in a place of paralyzing discouragement was not the solution. He knew that the victory He had planned for Joshua required him to dust off the self-pity.

2. **There is something you need to fix.**

God reminded Joshua that there were problems that had to be addressed before God would move on behalf of Israel. Then God gave Joshua a new strategy, one that reflected God's leadership and timing.

3. **Go back and fight.**

God asked Joshua to return to the place of defeat and fight the battle again God's way. This time, He promised victory, and victory is what He delivered.

That, friends, is also God's promise to us when defeat threatens to paralyze us. Defeat is never the end of the story when we follow the wisdom of God's word. It is often where we learn our most valuable lessons, where we discover our strength, and where God breeds our most profound victories.

I finished the year at country school, and I am so thankful God wouldn't let me quit in the middle of my defeat. I would love to tell you that, after I picked myself up, got a new strategy more aligned with God's will, and went back to fight again that the victory was easy. It was not.

But I did experience victory. God used my defeat to show me that I was stronger and more resourceful than I ever dreamed. I learned the value of perseverance and humility. The teaching and management skills I learned because I had to survive became the foundation for many years in the classroom and as a principal. God even used the wisdom from that experience at pivotal moments in my career to remind me that I am not a quitter.

If defeat is taunting you right now, I pray you will hear God's voice encouraging you. He has big plans for this temporary setback, and He always has the last word. So, dust off your discouragement, allow Him to give you a new strategy, and get back to the fight. He has a huge victory waiting for you.

Dear Victorious Father,

I am so thankful that You don't just promise me victory, You deliver it. Even though I feel discouraged and scared, I trust You to bring victory out of this defeat. Help me dust off my self-pity. Show me anything in my life that is getting in the way and help me remove it. Give me courage to go back into battle, following You and trusting Your promise for victory. In Jesus' name, Amen.

REFLECTIONS

1. Where do you feel God asking you to "stand up"? Identify any areas of discouragement that are holding you down.

2. Ask God to give you a new strategy for victory in your battle. Write down any thoughts He gives you.

3. Spend time this week recalling previous defeats that God has turned into victories for you.

Scriptures

"The Lᴏʀᴅ gives strength to his people. The Lᴏʀᴅ blesses his people with peace."

—Psalm 29:11

"What, then, shall we say in response to these things? If God is for us, who can be against us? He who did not spare his own Son, but gave him up for us all—how will he not also, along with him, graciously give us all things?…No, in all these things we are more than conquerors through him who loved us."

—Romans 8:31–32, 37

"But thanks be to God! He gives us the victory through our Lord Jesus Christ."

—1 Corinthians 15:57

Help for Stressful Times
I DON'T EVEN KNOW MY NAME

Life as an elementary school principal was often stressful, but that day was one of the worst. Impossible deadlines loomed. Challenging behaviors kept me sprinting from crisis to crisis. An angry parent stormed my office and demanded an immediate solution to a problem I hadn't created. And a staff member's decision left me scrambling to bring order from the chaos it caused.

The high school my daughter attended sat across the highway from the elementary school, and her school day ended an hour before ours. She rode the bus over every day and hung out in the office area doing homework until I finished my day. Most days she stopped by my office just to say hello, but on that particular day, for some reason she added a question. "Hey Mom, what's for dinner?" The answer to her innocent question spilled out of my mouth with much more force than I'd intended. "How can I possibly know what's for dinner?" I snapped. "I don't even know my *name* right now!"

You know that feeling. Stress is embedded into the fiber of teaching, and usually we are okay with that. But the chronic stress of impossible expectations, challenging behaviors, and decisions outside our control can swirl around us like the waves of a storm at sea, burying us under the weight of stress and washing away the joy of our calling to teach.

If you are struggling with the storm of stress right now, I hope you find encouragement and peace in the story of Jesus in the storm on the Sea of Galilee. Matthew, Mark, and Luke all tell the story, but I love how Mark's version (4:35–41) emphasizes the teaching heart of Jesus. He had taught the crowds for days, and He asked His disciples to take Him across the sea. Almost as soon as they left the shore, He fell asleep on a cushion in the stern of the boat. While He slept, a fierce storm came up that threatened to break the boat apart. Terrified, the disciples woke Jesus up with this question, "Teacher, don't you care if we drown?" (v 4:38). Jesus got up, spoke to the waves, and immediately peace was restored.

There is a lot of encouragement for me in this story, especially during times of extreme stress. It brings me peace to be reminded that Jesus was a teacher and in His humanity, teaching exhausted Him so completely that He slept through a storm violent enough to frighten the veteran seamen on board. I find strength in knowing that He understands how exhausting the stress of teaching can be. He's been there. He knows.

But the real victory in this story for our own stressful times is the power Jesus has over the storm. When we are in trouble, fighting wave after wave on our own, struggling against forces more powerful than our human ability to cope, we can cry out to Him. He cares. He has both the desire and the power to quiet our storm. In His strongest teacher voice, He tells those misbehaving waves to sit down and be quiet. Then, like He did with the disciples, He leads us beyond the storm to the other side of the sea so we can continue our work for Him.

So…maybe when I am stressed beyond my ability to cope, I don't have to know *my* name. My power to overcome is in knowing the name of the One who "even the winds and the waves obey." My survival is in the hands of Jesus, the One who can bring peace to my heart just by the words He speaks.

This week, let's call on that name. Let's remember that Jesus knows what we are going through and won't let the waves destroy us. Let's hold on to His power in the face of the fiercest winds and trust Him to calm our spirit and strengthen our faith to continue His work beyond the storm.

Dear Storm-Quieting Father,

Stress is no joke. I'm fighting a battle against it this week, but I don't want to fight on my own. I'm calling on *Your name* and asking for Your help. I believe You know what I'm going through, that You care, and that You have the power to speak to the winds and waves of my storm. Strengthen my faith to continue the work You have called me to. In Jesus' name, Amen.

REFLECTIONS

1. What is causing you to "not know your own name" this week? Be specific and write down what God brings to your mind.

2. How have you tried to fight stress in your own strength?

3. What differences do you notice when you call on Jesus' name to calm your stress storm?

SCRIPTURES

"The LORD himself goes before you and will be with you; he will never leave you or forsake you."

—Deuteronomy 31:8

"He got up, rebuked the wind and said to the waves, 'Quiet! Be still!' Then the wind died down and it was completely calm."

—Mark 4:39

"I have told you these things, so that in me you may have peace. In this world you will have trouble. But take heart! I have overcome the world."

—John 16:33

Under the Broom Bush

GOD'S RESPONSE WHEN I'VE HAD ENOUGH

• • • •

"Okay, that's it! I'm done!" I sat staring at my test scores, on the low side of abysmal, and I could barely catch my breath. I was humiliated. Defeated. Completely confused because I had done everything I knew to do. My only intention in that moment was to turn in my resignation as soon as I could type it.

Like you, I have experienced many times in teaching when I felt like I lived on top of the world. Times when I felt like I was exactly where God wanted me to be, doing exactly what He had called me to do. I've experienced the luxury of deeply satisfying and meaningful work and the indescribable joy of investing in the lives of students. But there are other times—like that day—when I had come to the end of my resources. Times when exhaustion and emptiness made me sit down and say, "I've had enough!"

Has giving up crossed your mind this week? Are you feeling tired and empty? Are you ready to tell God you've had enough? If that's not you this week, skip this one, or read it to encourage a friend. But if it does describe you, jump in with me and let's look at how our God responds when we can't take another step.

Our encouragement is found in the story of Elijah. This

mighty prophet had spent his life working for God, dedicated to speaking God's truth during difficult times. His relationship with God was intimate and personal, and his ministry was marked with powerful victories. But he came to a time when he was so tired and so depleted, he was ready to quit.

"Elijah was afraid and ran for his life…He came to a broom bush, sat down under it and prayed that he might die. 'I have had enough, Lord,' he said" (1 Kings 19:3–4).

I love that our human imperfections are mirrored in the pages of Scripture. When we are ready to give up on something God has called us to, we can go to Scripture and find someone who felt the same way. Elijah had experienced amazing displays of God's power. Yet, when he was at the end of his own resources, he begged God to let him quit.

I find comfort in Elijah's human limitations. But I find hope and power in the divinely perfect love of God. It is encouraging to me that God doesn't expect us to be on top of the mountain all the time. He knows there will be times when we will come to our own form of a broom bush, sit down, and beg Him to let us out of the assignment He has given us.

Look at God's response to Elijah's request. "All at once an angel touched him and said, 'Get up and eat.' He looked around, and there by his head was some bread baked over hot coals, and a jar of water. He ate and drank and then lay down again" (1 Kings 19:5–6).

In God's love for Elijah, He didn't scold him or shame him. He loved him. He fed him. Then he let him rest. God understood Elijah's humanness and met him at his exact point of need. In fact, He fed him twice! "The angel of the

Lord came back a second time and touched him and said, 'Get up and eat, for the journey is too much for you'" (1 Kings 19:7).

As a teacher, you get it that Elijah was too tired to eat, and that he was so empty the angel had to feed him twice. You understand that kind of emptiness and exhaustion. God knows that. He sees exactly where you are and knows exactly what you need, and He will go to great lengths to meet you and give you the nourishment and rest you need.

Verse 8 may be my favorite: "Strengthened by that food, he traveled forty days and forty nights" (1 Kings 19:8). God had more for Elijah to do, so what He gave him under that tree didn't just meet his current need for refreshment. It also gave him the strength for his next assignment.

God met me under my own broom bush, an umbrella at the beach, where I had gone to decide about quitting. He had more for me to do, and under that umbrella, He gave me everything I needed to go back and try again. He didn't want me quitting in defeat. He wanted me to allow Him to give me what I needed to complete the job I had been called to do.

God has more for you too. He sees your human heart that is running on empty, and He knows you've had enough. This week, will you let Him meet you under your broom bush? Will you trust that He will nourish you and strengthen you for the important work He has for you? Will you open your eyes to what He lovingly provides?

Dear Strengthening Father,

I admit it. I am ready to quit. I know You have work for me to do. I know You are faithful and have been with me every step of my journey. But right now, I can't go another step without Your intervention. Lord, find me under this bush and give me what I need to go on. Minister to me like You did to Elijah. My soul needs nourishment and rest, and I know You will provide. The enemy would love to see me quit, but I trust You to give me the strength I need to finish strong for You. In Jesus' name, Amen.

REFLECTIONS

1. In what area of your life have you had enough? What are you tempted to quit?

2. Can you find time this week to meet with God under your broom bush? Tell Him how you are feeling. Ask Him for what you need.

3. Look for all the ways God ministers to you this week. Look for the angels He sends, the bread baked over hot coals, the water, the rest. How can you open your eyes and heart and gain strength from His loving provision?

SCRIPTURES

"The angel of the LORD encamps around those who fear him, and he delivers them."
—Psalm 34:7

"So do not fear, for I am with you; do not be dismayed, for I am your God. I will strengthen you and help you; I will uphold you with my righteous right hand."
—Isaiah 41:10

"Come to me, all you who are weary and burdened, and I will give you rest. Take my yoke upon you and learn from me, for I am gentle and humble in heart, and you will find rest for your souls."

—Matthew 11:28–29

Moving in Gods Timing
TRUSTING THE WAIT

•———— • • • • ————•

The student at the microphone was passionate about the message in his solo, and his deep, soulful voice filled the auditorium. His timing, however, was awful. Every time he opened his mouth to sing, he started two or three beats ahead of the music. Honestly, it was like listening to fingernails on a chalkboard. The music teacher frantically exaggerated her movements to get him to start on the downbeat, but he jumped in early every time. The confused musicians and back-up vocalists scrambled to follow his lead, but after several attempts to adjust their accompaniment to his bad timing, they gave up. Without musical support, the song was weak and awkward. Rushing ahead of the song's timing seriously undermined its power.

On the way home that night, God gently reminded me that sometimes my timing is off too. I can get in a big hurry to have situations go my way, and I get locked into a rhythm of expectation and disappointment. I sometimes rush into a situation with passion but fall flat because, in my haste, I run ahead of God's support. Sometimes, I feel more stress than necessary because I'm not trusting the power and promise of God to direct my life.

Do you struggle with waiting on God's timing? Does impatience tempt you when He asks you to wait for that relationship to be restored? Or an illness to be healed? Or a dream to be realized? Or when you need deliverance from a difficult situation?

Teachers understand timing. We know its importance when introducing concepts, asking strategic questions, intervening in conflicts, communicating with parents. We see the critical difference timing makes for our students, but when we are asked to wait on God, it can be so hard. I look at difficult situations in my life, and I can't understand why God doesn't seem to be moving NOW! I've prayed expectantly and passionately, and now I want God to move on my schedule. When He doesn't, I'm tempted to rush in and try to fix what only He can fix. Or I'm tempted to stop praying and stop trusting because I've grown tired of waiting on Him. But when I rush ahead of His timing, His power gets diminished, and my life becomes like that awkward song—full of potential but weak and powerless.

That is not what I want my life to be, and I don't want it for you, either. So this week, while we wait, I invite you to claim these promises:

1. Ecclesiastes 3:11 promises that "God has made everything beautiful in its time." This week, let's believe that there is some beauty in everything we face, and at the perfect time, God will reveal its beauty to us.

2. Isaiah 40:31 promises that "Those who wait on the Lord will renew their strength" (NKJV). This week, let's believe that God is strengthening us during our waiting time, teaching us lessons we could never learn if everything came quickly or easily.

3. Lamentations 3:24–26 promises that "the LORD is good to those who wait for Him, to the soul who seeks Him" (NKJV). Because the God we serve has already made everything beautiful, let's trust His timing. Let's keep our eyes on Him and trust Him to tell us exactly when to wait and when to move. Let's seek His will more than His provision. And let's watch for His goodness toward us while we wait.

4. Ephesians 3:20 promises that God is, "able to do immeasurably more than all we ask or imagine, according to his power that is at work within us." This week, let's believe that, if God is not answering our prayers in the way we want or in the time we want, then He must have something far better in mind for us than we can even imagine. He loves us too much to withhold His best, and we can trust that His best is worth the wait.

There is a happy ending to the choir story. A few days after that nightmare rehearsal, our choir performed their song for parents. The music teacher had worked with our young soloist and coached him to keep his eyes on her and to trust that she would tell him exactly when to start singing. This time, he waited, and the song was magical. Its power swept through the audience and brought them to their feet, many of them in tears because the message of the song touched their hearts. The difference was in trusting the wait.

Dear Perfectly On-Time Father,

You know how hard it is for me to trust Your timing, especially when You ask me to wait. But I don't want my life to be weak and powerless because I rush ahead of You.

Teach me to trust Your timing. Help me to remember that Your best for me is greater than anything I can ask You for, and that it will always come right on time. Make my life a powerful testimony to Your beauty and goodness. In Jesus' name, Amen.

REFLECTIONS

1. Think of a situation in your life where God is asking you to wait on His timing.

2. How does the truth in the promises of God in this week's devotion change your perspective on the wait?

3. Look for ways God is being good to you while you wait for Him. Journal what you notice.

SCRIPTURES

"I remain confident of this: I will see the goodness of the LORD in the land of the living. Wait for the LORD; be strong and take heart and wait for the LORD."
   —Psalm 27:13–14

"For the revelation awaits an appointed time; it speaks of the end and will not prove false. Though it linger, wait for it; it will certainly come and will not delay."
   —Habakkuk 2:3

"Let us not become weary in doing good, for at the proper time we will reap a harvest if we do not give up."
   —Galatians 6:9

Part Four:
Choosing Empowerment

Knowing What I Have Control Over

Guarding Our Thoughts
YOU'RE DRIVING ON THE SIDEWALK!

• • • •

After eighteen years in the classroom, I headed back to school for certification as an administrator. Driving around the unfamiliar campus, I could see the administration building in the distance, but no road I took got me closer.

Eventually, an open gate and a cobblestone road that looked like it led in the right direction invited me to turn onto it. I wondered out loud what the gate was for and why the roads on campus were so narrow, but I kept driving. After a few seconds, I saw someone walking on the road in my direction, so I stopped, lowered my window, and asked if he knew how to get to the Admin Building. "Sure, I can tell you how to get there," he said, "but you can't get there from here. You are you driving on the sidewalk!"

God has a reason for everything that happens to us, and beyond His obvious efforts to keep me humble, He allowed that phrase to stick in my head. Driving on the sidewalk has become a metaphor for any time I am stuck on a path that leads nowhere. An enticing but frustrating path where I can see my destination but can't reach it because I am mindlessly following a dead-end.

You know where I spend the most time driving on sidewalks in my life? Where I waste time and energy going nowhere and embarrass myself at what little impact I have?

Where I am defeated before I even get started and often have to reverse my direction and find a better path? For me, it is what I allow inside my head. What I think about. What about you? Do your thoughts ever keep you on a road to nowhere?

1. You long to renew your joy and passion for teaching but get stuck in thoughts of discouragement and despair.

2. You delight in creativity but allow thoughts of envy or bitterness to occupy the spaces in your mind where solutions are meant to grow.

3. You imagine being a world-changer but get lost in thoughts of rejection, inferiority, and "what ifs."

4. You desire deep connections with other teachers but allow thoughts of comparison and criticism to steer you away from meaningful relationships.

5. You have inspiring dreams but hang out on the perfection sidewalk and never take the first step.

King Solomon, the wisest man to ever live, knew the power of thoughts. He knew that what we think about influences every decision and that walking into what God has for us requires being very careful about what we allow to happen inside our heads. In a heart-to-heart talk with his son, he shared this wisdom: "Above all else, guard your heart, for everything you do flows from it" (Prov 4:23).

Can you hear our own heavenly Father's concern for us echoed in the words of Solomon to his son? What we hold in our heart begins with a thought, so God places a high priority on watching what we think about. We reflect His heart when our thoughts move us forward to accomplish His mission for teaching.

Guarding our hearts starts with simple awareness, so this week, let's pay more attention to our thoughts. When students cross your mind as you fall asleep, what are your thoughts? When a new strategy is introduced in the staff meeting, what are your thoughts? When your principal asks you to lead your team next year, what are your thoughts? When going back to school for an advanced degree becomes a possibility, what are your thoughts? When a colleague makes a rude remark about you, what are your thoughts?

In the teaching world, we are often tempted to turn onto sidewalks of thoughts that take us in circles. But we have a destination to reach. We have a destiny to fulfill. So this week, let's become more aware of the thoughts we entertain. Let's do what we teach our students to do: let's think about what we're thinking about. Let's ask God to tenderly reveal to us which thoughts keep us on the road to a destiny of greatness and which ones keep us driving on a sidewalk to nowhere.

Dear Destiny-Guiding Father,

Thank You for loving me and for creating me to do great things in Your Name. I know that my thoughts are powerful because You say they influence every decision. Please help me be aware of my thoughts and show me where my thoughts bring You glory and where You want to give me more of the "mind of Christ." This week, Lord, I invite You to search my thoughts because I trust that You love me and want me to walk in Your truth. In Jesus' name, Amen.

REFLECTIONS

1. Pay attention to your thoughts this week. What are some of your default thoughts, the ones that immediately come to mind when you face a challenge?

2. Trace one outcome of your life this week back to its originating thought. Did the thought reflect God's heart for your work?

3. Ask God to show you how your thoughts are influencing your destiny to live a life that gives Him glory.

SCRIPTURES

"Let the words of my mouth and the meditation of my heart be acceptable in Your sight O LORD, my Rock and my Redeemer."
—Psalm 19:14

"Test me, LORD, and try me, examine my heart and my mind; for I have always been mindful of your unfailing love and have lived in reliance on your faithfulness."
—Psalm 26:2–3

"Jesus replied: 'Love the Lord your God with all your heart and with all your soul and with all your mind.' This is the first and greatest commandment."
—Matthew 22:37–38

Thoughts Grounded in Truth
RUNNING TO WIN

Chatting and squirming, my fourth graders found their places and waited for the signal to start the half-mile Field Day race. Brock, a capable runner, began the race with his classmates, but as the race continued, he fell farther and farther behind. When the kids rounded the track for their final lap, he was almost a full lap behind the leader.

I knew he could run. I had watched him at recess. Thinking that maybe he didn't feel well, I fell in beside him on his last lap. We jogged only a few yards together before I knew he was okay, so I asked if he wanted to pick up the pace and catch up with his classmates. "Nah, Mrs. Tidwell," he said. "I'm thinking that, at any minute, they'll blow the whistle to run the other direction, and when they do, I'll be in first place."

I didn't know what to say to that, so I jogged with him across the finish line where he finished dead last. After a couple minutes of rest and a few gulps of water, I couldn't resist asking, "Brock, what were you thinking?"

"In class, the teacher blows his whistle and makes us run the other way," he said, "and I thought he would do that today."

After a quick reminder that Field Day events and class

runs are different, he trotted off to join his classmates for their next event, fairly unfazed by his defeat. But I sat on the playground bench processing some bigger life lessons I had just learned from that spunky kid. Brock came in last in a race he could have won, and it was his thoughts, not his ability nor his circumstances, that lost the race for him that day. More than that, his unsuccessful race strategy was based entirely on a thought not grounded in truth.

I don't want to run my race that way, do you? If my thoughts determine whether I win or lose, I want to choose winning thoughts. I don't want my race sabotaged by thoughts that deceive me and entice me to run a sloppy, uninspired race. I want to run to win! If choosing victory-producing thoughts sounds good to you, I invite you to look with me at the truth of two Scriptures. One teaches us thoughts that sabotage, and one teaches thoughts that win races.

Ephesians 4:31: "Get rid of all bitterness, rage and anger, brawling and slander, along with every form of malice."

Scripture says that resentful, angry, slanderous thoughts don't make for a good race strategy. God doesn't say we won't ever have those thoughts. He says to get rid of them before they sabotage our race. When we cling to thoughts of bitterness and rehearse hurts over and over, we lose sight of the finish line. We forget that we are running a race of purpose. When we hold onto thoughts of anger and slander, it depletes our energy and trips up those who run with us. No one wins when arguing and rage control our thoughts.

But God wants us to win, so in the last phrase of the passage, He lays out the strategy. Get rid of every form of malice—that means every thought that reflects any desire to cause pain and suffering to ourselves or others. It's not easy to do, but we are more likely to win when we don't carry the extra weight.

> Philippians 4:8: "Finally, brothers and sisters, whatever is true, whatever is noble, whatever is right, whatever is pure, whatever is lovely, whatever is admirable—if anything is excellent or praiseworthy—think about such things."

Now that's a race strategy. God says simply, "Think about such things." Does that feel as empowering to you as it does to me? I have a choice of what I think about. You may not find that as refreshing as I do because you have already learned to fill your mind with the kind of thoughts that move you forward. But knowing that my thoughts are borne out of my own choices is empowering to me. It makes me feel lighter, less encumbered. It gives me hope and direction. Thinking God's way liberates me from thoughts that sabotage my race and instead opens my mind to allow God to download fresh solutions and powerful possibilities. All my energy is freed up so I can run my race to win.

Teaching is a race God has called us to run. And it's a race we must win. The stakes are high. We run for our students' hearts and minds. We run to motivate and to inspire. We run to change lives, change families. We run to expose and develop potential. We run to shape the next generation.

This week, let's be intentional about our race strategy, choosing our thoughts based on the truths of Scripture. Let's deliberately get rid of thoughts that weigh us down and replace them with thoughts that make us winners. This week let's run this race to win it!

Dear Race-Empowering Father,

I start this prayer with confession, Lord. Only You know the time, relationships, and opportunities I have squandered because of thoughts that are contrary to Your will for me. Forgive me and help me change the way I think. When thoughts of malice come into my mind, help me get rid of them instantly, replacing them with what You tell me to think about. I want to run this race to win, but I need Your help every minute. In Jesus' name, Amen.

REFLECTIONS

1. Will the statement, "Our thoughts have more influence on our outcomes than our abilities and circumstances," affect the way you do your work this week? How?

2. Is there anything on the list from Ephesians 4:31 that God is nudging you to get rid of? How is that thought pattern sabotaging your victory?

3. Deliberately choose to replace any malicious or unproductive thoughts with thoughts from the list in Philippians 4:8. Journal anything you notice. Was it difficult? Did it change a negative attitude? Did it open up new possibilities for forward movement?

SCRIPTURES

"You will keep in perfect peace those whose minds are steadfast, because they trust in you."
—Isaiah 26:3

"Those who live according to the flesh have their minds set on what the flesh desires; but those who live in accordance with the Spirit have their minds set on what the Spirit desires. The mind governed by the flesh is death, but the mind governed by the Spirit is life and peace."

—Romans 8:5–6

"Do you not know that in a race all the runners run, but only one gets the prize? Run in such a way as to get the prize. Everyone who competes in the games goes into strict training. They do it to get a crown that will not last, but we do it to get a crown that will last forever."

—1 Corinthians 9:24–25

Reflecting God's Heart in the Words We Speak

POWER OF LIFE AND DEATH

"The tongue has the power of life and death . . ."
—Proverbs 18:21

Situation 1: A parent sat on the other side of my desk, furious about the consequences of his son's playground fight. He had already decided to move his child to a different school but insisted on an appointment with me before leaving. I don't remember a lot of what he said, but his parting words, thrown like a hatchet, have stuck in my mind for years. "The best part about leaving here is that I will never have to see your face again!"

Situation 2: A year and a half after retiring, I was asked to take an interim principal position for a school whose principal relocated in late fall. I was nervous after having been away from a school setting so long, but in my first week there, I knew I would be okay. The kids wrote welcome letters, wishing me luck as their new principal. I saved every letter because the words refreshed my soul. But these words from a first grader have echoed in my heart time and time again as pure life, "Dear Mrs. Tidwell, You will be loved here!"

Two extremes. Two outcomes. Each story a reminder of the truth of Proverbs 18:21.

The angry parent spoke death that day—maybe just the death of my ego and the belief that I could please everyone—but after all this time, I have not forgotten how his words hurt or how I doubted my ability to lead after that encounter. The first grader spoke life, and even now, when I think about her letter, my heart smiles, and I feel the fresh power of life in her words.

Spoken words really do have power, and each one of you could tell your own stories when the words of others have enriched your life or destroyed a piece of your heart. It seems that everyone has an opinion about what teachers do, and since our culture gives permission to speak before words are filtered, we are often the object of words that break our hearts. But can we take our focus off the words of others this week and allow God to speak to us about what comes out of our own mouths?

As educators, we speak thousands of words each day. If *every* word carries potential for building up and *every* word carries the potential for tearing down, that's a lot of power we wield.

1. Do we use our power to bring joy to others by choosing words of affirmation, healing, and hope or do we destroy joy by speaking harsh, sarcastic, and judgmental words?

2. Do we use the power of our words to preserve the dignity of others even when we talk about someone who is not in our presence, or do we destroy the reputation of

others by repeating reckless gossip or whispering criticism?

3. Do we empower our own lives by speaking words of expectation and purpose or do we waste our potential with words of grumbling, complaining, and despair?

I don't know about you, but I am not completely pleased with my own answers to these questions. I sense God calling me higher. I hear Him asking me to choose my words more carefully, more powerfully. I acknowledge His invitation to make my words more reflective of His heart. What about you? Is God nudging you to use your own words to create more life? Is He inviting you to reflect His graciousness more through the words you choose?

Will you join me this week in taking small steps toward transforming the power of the words that come out of our mouths? Let's begin by just being more *aware* of the words we speak. Let's listen to ourselves as an observer. Let's watch the reactions of others as our words reach their ears. Let's imagine the reactions of others as we speak about them when they can't hear us. Let's ask God to work on our hearts so our words can come from a place of His gracious love.

Don't worry if you don't get it all right this week. Speak kindly to yourself as well. Remember, you will be loved here.

Dear Life-Speaking Father,

Thank You for speaking words of life through Your Scripture and for reminding me of the awesome power for life or death in the thousands of words I speak each day. I want to use my words for the power of life, but it's not easy. There is a lot going on around me that tempts me to speak harsh, critical, disheartening words. Help me become more aware of the power in the words I speak and help me use my power to create life in myself and in those I serve. In Jesus' name, Amen.

REFLECTIONS

1. What do you notice about the power of your own words this week?

2. How is God speaking to you about how your words are affecting the outcome of your own life? The hearts of others?

3. Choose a situation where you typically respond with destructive words. Try altering your response by choosing words with the power of life. Did using your power for life change how you feel about the situation?

SCRIPTURES

"Those who guard their lips preserve their lives, but those who speaks rashly will come to ruin."
—Proverbs 13:3

"A good man brings good things out of the good stored up in his heart, and an evil man brings evil things out of the evil stored up in his heart. For the mouth speaks what the heart is full of."
—Luke 6:45

"Therefore, rid yourselves of all malice and all deceit, hypocrisy, envy, and slander of every kind."
—1 Peter 2:1

Higher than Complaining
MY DEAD BATTERY

* * * *

"Do everything without complaining . . ."
—Philippians 2:14 (NLT)

At twenty-three-years old, teaching Native American children in South Dakota was my dream job. Moving from Tennessee in August, I had already fallen in love with the kids and the culture. But on the day I flew back, after having Christmas with my family in Tennessee, I wasn't sure I would survive the climate.

Fifteen minutes before landing, the pilot announced that it was nine degrees on the ground in Sioux Falls with twenty-mile-per-hour winds, so I already dreaded the icy walk to the parking lot and the frigid car waiting for me to make the two-hour trip to my apartment.

I saw it when I opened the car door to put my luggage in the back seat—a flat tire, frozen to the icy parking lot surface. Unsure what would happen if I tried to jack up the car with the tire frozen to the ground, I decided to start the car and let it warm up while I thought of a plan. Sliding into freezing leather seats, I turned the ignition. Nothing. Not a sound. While my car sat in the parking lot for eight days, the subzero South Dakota temperatures had drained every ounce of life from my battery.

I had several choices at that moment. I could have sat in

my car thinking of ways to solve my problem. I could have gone back in the airport to ask for help. I could have walked to the gas station I could see from the parking lot. But I made an odd choice. I started complaining. Out loud. To no one! There I sat, alone and freezing, complaining about leaving my job in Tennessee, about the cold weather, and about my stupid dead battery. Honestly, complaining felt good for a few minutes, but eventually, I noticed something. I still had to teach the next day, I was freezing, my tire was still flat, and my dead battery was just as dead as it had been thirty minutes earlier.

You are probably a much better problem-solver than I was, but I suspect that you, too, have moments when you are tempted to complain.

1. When you've taken in half the kids from your teammate's class for the third day this week because she is sick and there are no subs.

2. When the state teacher evaluation changes and you spend all night preparing to hit twelve domains in one lesson observation.

3. When the troubled child in your room has just triggered a room clear for the twentieth time.

There is no judgment here. There is plenty to complain about in our profession. And frankly, sometimes we feel the need to vent. But, just like my airport experience, complaining rarely solves problems, rarely moves us forward, and rarely unlocks creative thinking. Most of the time, it is just a waste of time and words. And more than that, God calls us to rise above the temptation to complain because He wants our words to reflect His heart.

Hear His love as He invites us to go higher:

> "Do everything without complaining and arguing, so that no one can criticize you. Live clean, innocent lives as children of God, shining like bright lights in a world full of crooked and perverse people. Hold firmly to the word of life . . ." (Phil 2:14–16a, NLT).

God's invitation for us to do our work without complaining is an invitation to show His love to those around us, shining like stars in a culture where words of promise and purpose are so desperately needed. It is a reminder that we are His children with access to His hope and power in the most challenging times. It is a call to speak life instead of echoing the words of desperation and discouragement that seem to come so easily in the work we do.

This week, I want to go higher, and I invite you to join me. Let's ask God to show us where we waste precious time and energy complaining, and how we can channel those resources toward solutions. Let's walk away from conversations that dim our star power and tempt us to feed into desperation. Let's hold out words of life when things look hopeless because we know that we serve a God of hope. Let's reflect the heart of the God we serve and stand out against the culture as we lay those unvoiced complaints at His feet.

Dear Problem-Solving Father,

Thank You for Your word that calls me to rise above the waste of complaining. You want me to spend my life making a difference, so please show me how to shine like a star even when those around me speak words of desperation. Help me to be more like You so that when I speak, I create life with my words. In Jesus' name, Amen.

REFLECTIONS

1. Listen to your words this week and notice any waste of complaining.

2. Notice opportunities this week where you can "shine like a star" in difficult situations.

3. What word of life would you like to hold out to those around you? How will you let others see the power of God working through your adversity?

SCRIPTURES

"The words of the reckless pierce like swords, but the tongue of the wise brings healing."
    —Proverbs 12:18

"Ah, Sovereign LORD, you have made the heavens and the earth by your great power and outstretched arm. Nothing is too hard for you."
    —Jeremiah 32:17

"Be very careful, then, how you live—not as unwise but as wise, making the most of every opportunity, because the days are evil. Therefore do not be foolish, but understand what the Lord's will is."
    —Ephesians 5:15–17

The Power of Encouragement
WE BELIEVE IN YOU

• — • • • • — •

Just days after the state test scores came out, I received a phone call late in the afternoon "inviting" me to central office the next morning. My directions were to be ready to discuss the reasons our scores were low and to outline our plan for improving them. Sleep was sporadic that night. Thoughts of other jobs I could do when they fired me the next day kept me tossing all night.

Six central office department heads were seated at the conference table looking very serious when I walked in the next morning. I braced myself for impact knowing I was about to lose my job, but the first words I heard changed everything. "We believe in you!" were the words that opened the meeting.

I spent the next hour and a half answering three questions: What is your plan? What do you need? How can we help? I still can't say that was an enjoyable meeting, but I left it feeling empowered, and, like throwing a stone in a lake, their encouragement to me had a ripple effect on our entire school family. A short two years later, our school community made so much academic growth, we were *rewarded* for our scores.

No wonder the Apostle Paul gave such a clear directive in his letter to the Thessalonian church: "Encourage one another and build each other up . . ." (1 Thes 5:11). Encouragement is powerful. Can you imagine the ripple effect that would be unleashed if encouragement became a daily part of our routine? Look at what Scripture says about the power of encouragement.

Encouragement reflects the heart of God—Our God is a God of encouragement, and He calls us to glorify Him by doing the same for each other. When we encourage, we reflect the love of God who speaks tender encouraging words into us. When that love is reflected through us, those around us are drawn to God. (Romans 15:4)

Encouragement inspires—My defeated attitude was transformed into inspiration by four words of encouragement: "We believe in you." When we help others see new possibilities, when we challenge them to grow, when we let them know that we see more in them than they see in themselves, we lift them up where they can get a better view of their own potential. (Ecclesiastes 4:10)

Encouragement unifies—When we come alongside each other with words like, "How can I help?" it unites us and reminds us that we are family. The success of everyone in the family is important because we are all working toward the same mission. (Romans 15:5)

Encouragement empowers—Powerful encouragement goes beyond flattering words. It doesn't gloss over imperfections; it works to help solve problems. Questions like: "What do you need?" help to re-

focus on goals and a plan for reaching those goals.
(Proverbs 16:23)

I think most of us would agree that our profession needs the power of encouragement. We need inspiration. We need to feel empowered. We need to feel the unity of accomplishing something bigger than any of us could do alone. Many educators wrestle with leaving the profession every year. Discouragement is widespread. In fact, I can almost hear your own tired heart asking how you can receive desperately needed words of encouragement.

I have two promises to share with you. First, we serve an encouraging God who will see that we receive the encouragement we need to do the job He calls us to do. The second promise is this: "From the fruit of their lips people are filled with good things, and the work of their hands brings them reward" (Prov 12:14).

Our own needs for encouragement will be filled when we speak encouragement to others. Our words will come back to us. Isn't that a great promise? The more we encourage each other, the more encouragement we will receive.

So, this week, let's go all out. Let's remember that God gives encouragement, and we glorify Him when we do the same. Let's actively seek out students, colleagues, families, and leaders who need words of affirmation, and let's give them a glimpse of their own potential for greatness. Let's be on the lookout for those in our school family who need our help, who need us to work with them and help them reach for ever higher goals. Let's bring unity into our family by actively working for everyone's success. And let's pause when someone encourages us and thank God for His promise to fill us with good things when we use our words to reflect His heart.

Dear Encouraging Father,

Thank You for the kind words of others that fill my heart with encouragement and inspiration. Help me be the kind of person who builds others up with my words. I want to reflect Your heart with inspiring, empowering, unifying words. It's not always easy to speak those words when I need them myself. But I know that You will fill me with the encouragement I need when I speak those words to others. In Jesus' name, Amen.

REFLECTIONS

1. How can you inspire someone this week with encouraging words?

2. Is there someone in your school who needs your help and your practical advice to solve a problem? How can you reach out to him/her this week?

3. Notice the encouragement you receive this week. How does it inspire and empower you?

SCRIPTURES

"The mouth of the righteous is a fountain of life, but the mouth of the wicked conceals violence."
—Proverbs 10:11

"Do not let any unwholesome talk come out of your mouths, but only what is helpful for building others up according to their needs, that it may benefit those who listen."

— Ephesians 4:29

"But encourage one another daily, as long as it is called 'Today,' so that none of you may be hardened by sin's deceitfulness."

— Hebrews 3:13

Part Five:

PLEADING FOR GOD'S HELP

SEEKING DIVINE GUIDANCE AND INTERVENTION

Power of Prayer
LINES ON THE ROAD

• • • •

South Dakota winters are brutal. Bitter cold and tons of snow. But even though it snowed almost every week, school was rarely canceled due to weather. Level roads were plowed quickly, and it was possible, even with several inches of snow, for teachers and students to get to school. Except for blizzards. When icy winds swirled the snow across roads, driving was treacherous for everyone.

Six of us rode together from the town where we lived to the reservation where we taught, and everyone but me was an experienced winter driver. It wasn't my week to drive, so I was only a little nervous the morning we headed out in four inches of fresh snow with four more inches predicted during the day. Frigid temps made the snow light, and our road was freshly plowed, so no one in the car seemed concerned…until the wind picked up and the snow started swirling around us. By the time we found a place to turn around, the blowing snow had obscured every landmark, and white was all we could see.

This southern girl started to panic a little, but those hearty South Dakota travelers did something I will never forget. They opened the car doors, leaned out as far as they could, and started searching for the lines on the road. As the driver inched forward, they yelled, "You're getting off the road over here. Go left." "You're over the middle line, go to the right." All the way home, the lines on the road gave our driver direction to safely steer us out of that blinding snow and back to safety.

I rarely paid attention to the lines on the road until that day, but God used that experience to teach me about the power of prayer. He showed me that, like the lines on the road that guided our daily journey to and from school, constant communication with Him provides the guidance we need to make our life journey with confidence and direction. Then, in our most challenging situations, when we can't see what is ahead, when we are blinded by the swirling of overwhelming crisis, prayer is our lifeline.

Many times since that day, I have looked to the story of Hezekiah in 2 Kings for a reminder of the critical importance of prayer. Hezekiah was a godly king of Judah, but because previous kings had forsaken God, the kingdom needed redemption and restoration. Determined to bring his people back to God, Hezekiah relentlessly sought God's will daily to guide him, and through prayer, God steered the kingdom into peace and purpose.

Then Hezekiah's "blizzard" struck. A neighboring king sent a message that his large, bloodthirsty army was on its way to destroy Judah. Military leaders from the enemy's army were sent to taunt the people, predicting crushing defeat and unspeakable hardships. Hezekiah knew the power of his enemy, and he clearly understood the implications of defeat. With danger swirling around him, his human vision was obscured, but he knew how to find his way. Prayer.

Hezekiah "went up to the temple of the Lord and spread it out before the Lord" (2 Kings 19:14).

I love both parts of that verse. First, he went up to the temple. He got away from the noise and distraction of his predicament and went to a quiet place where he could hear from God. Then, he "spread it out before the Lord." He didn't give in to his blinding fear. He didn't wring his hands in defeat and spread his worry to those around him. He went to God and poured his heart out in prayer.

I hope that you can read all of Hezekiah's story this week in 2 Kings because he is such a great model for us as we navigate our teaching journey. Like Hezekiah, consistent prayer keeps our focus on God and opens our eyes to His daily direction. It allows us to see His way and hear His direction more clearly every day.

But when the blizzard hits—when a family's tragedy brings sudden behavior challenges, when a child moves in and throws a well-oiled classroom into mid-year chaos, when an administrator becomes demanding and distant, when sour and defeated colleagues threaten our sanity, when we lose our direction and can't envision teaching ever feeling safe again—prayer is our lifeline.

This week, let's seek God's direction through prayer. Let's find a quiet place where we can hear from the Lord. It may be the teacher's restroom stall. It may be a chapel. It may be behind the closed doors of our classroom while students are at the library. Whatever is going on, whether it is the daily need for guidance or a blinding blizzard of stress, let's spread it out before the Lord. Let's pray expectantly and boldly, trusting God to provide exactly what we need.

Dear Life-Steering Father,

I acknowledge that You made heaven and earth, and You alone are God. All the distractions to teaching and all the challenges I face every day are nothing compared to Your power. Hear me and see me and steer my life daily. And Lord, when the blizzard hits, be my deliverance. May Your truth, power, and love for me guide me through to safety so that those around me will know that You alone, O Lord, are God. In Jesus' name, Amen.

REFLECTIONS

1. How can you build in a few minutes each day to spend time with God so that He can direct Your life?

2. If you are experiencing a crisis (blizzard), how can you get away from the noise and get with God so that you can spread it out before the Lord?

3. Write down the ways God provides direction when You spend time with Him. Also, write down signs of His deliverance when you are threatened by crisis.

SCRIPTURES

"Look to the LORD and his strength; seek his face always."
—1 Chronicles 16:11

"Then you will call on me and come and pray to me, and I will listen to you."
—Jeremiah 29:12

"This is the confidence we have in approaching God: that if we ask anything according to his will, he hears us."

—1 John 5:14

Praying for Students
DON'T TAKE ANYTHING FOR GRANTED

• • • •

"You know the drill…Eat something healthy for breakfast. Be on time. Be ready. Tomorrow is testing day." My friend dismissed her students on the afternoon before the big test with one more request: "Get a good night's sleep tonight!"

As she stood at her classroom door the next morning to greet her students, she put a check beside each name on her attendance roster. Only one student missing. As she started to close the classroom door, she heard his uncontrollable sobs before he rounded the hallway corner. His words came between gasps making them almost impossible to understand. "Ms. Lynn. I can't take the test. I tried to get a good night's sleep like you said, but I was up all night. Somebody drove by and shot my neighbor. I couldn't sleep, Ms. Lynn, I'm sorry. I'm not ready for the test."

Telling me that story years after it happened, there was still pain in that teacher's eyes, but it was what she said next that captured my heart. "Before that happened," she said, "I just assumed everyone could get a good night's sleep, but I've never again taken anything for granted in my students' lives."

What a wakeup call. I thought about all the times I had taken for granted that each child was in a good learning space feeling safe, focused, and motivated. So many times I have forgotten that students experience the brokenness of society—conflict, confusion, violence, anxiety—and that brokenness is what often presents itself as distracted, disinterested, or disrespectful learners.

I could hear the unvoiced questions of students echoing through my head.

How can I focus on multiplication when my dad walked out this morning, and I have no idea if he is coming back?

How can writing possibly take center stage when my brother came home high for the fourth afternoon this week?

Why on earth would learning state capitals be important to me when we ran out of food, and I went to bed hungry?

How can you demand respect from me when tv sitcoms have been my babysitter since I was an infant?

I could go on and on and so could you. Frankly, it can be disheartening to stand in an environment of brokenness every day and remain committed to student success. But what if we stop taking anything for granted in our students' lives? What if we trust God when He tells us there is an enemy who fights every day for the minds and hearts of our students? And what if we fight back by bringing God's power into their lives?

How on earth do we fight, especially when those of us who work in public schools are legally restricted from talking to students about God? We fight back by talking to God about students. We pray for them. Like Hezekiah, we go "up to the temple of the Lord and spread it out before the Lord" on their behalf (2 Kings 19:14). God has no restrictions. He changes lives. He heals hearts. He overcomes the enemy. He brings purpose out of trauma. He guides, restores, and redeems.

Join with me this week, and let's fight on our knees for our kids, asking God to do what we can't. Let's boldly pray for God's protection and guidance in each child's life. Let's ask Him to fulfill destinies and use difficulties to strengthen and grow each child. Let's pray like the warriors God chose us to be, fighting for the destiny of each child as if he or she were our own.

I know many of you pray for your students and their specific needs, but I've written a few sample prayers for you to use if you need them. Pick and choose and personalize them for your students. But please pray. Our students need the mighty power of God in their lives so they can walk into the greatness He has planned for them.

Dear Child-Loving Father,

    Prayer for protection: I pray for Your protection over the hearts, minds, and lives of my students. I claim Your Word that you will protect them from the evil one (1 John 5:18), that You will be their hiding place when life is hard (Ps 32:7), and that You will be a refuge and tower of strength against the enemy of their souls (Ps 61:3).

    Prayer for purpose/destiny: You have created *all* my students for something special and wonderful (Eph

2:10). May they thirst for and pursue righteousness (2 Tim 2:22). May they hear You calling them to holy lives (2 Tim 1:9) and yield to Your will (Rom 6:13). May they accept Your gifts of open eyes to see You and open ears to hear You (Prov 20:12) and may every child walk into his or her destiny to be the salt of the earth and the light of the world (Matt 5:13).

Prayer for the minds of students: Satan works hard to capture young minds and much of what my students see and hear pollutes their minds and hijacks their thoughts. But You are greater than anything in this world (1 John 4:4) and Your desire is to give them a sound mind (2 Tim 1:7, NKJV). Please don't let them be blinded by the enemy, but let Your light shine in their hearts so their minds can be filled with the knowledge of You (2 Cor 4:4–5). Show them how to trust You (Isa 26:3) and let Your peace guard their hearts and minds (Phil 4:7).

Prayer for choices: Help my students make choices that bring life and blessings (Deut 31:19). Teach them to imitate what is good and not what is evil (1 John 2:15). Help them choose compassion and humility (1 Pet 3:8) and help them treat everyone with the respect and kindness they would want others to show to them (Matt 7:12).

Prayer during difficult times: Many of my students face challenges that I can't even imagine. I claim Your word over them today that You are close to the brokenhearted and You save those who are crushed in spirit (Ps 34:18). I acknowledge that You can redeem any situation, no matter how broken (Ex 6:6). When my students experience trauma, I pray that they will feel Your strong arms gently pulling them out of the pit and setting their feet on solid ground (Ps 40:2). Where the enemy plans harm, turn it into good for them (Gen 50:20). Where the enemy plans destruction, give them abundant life (John 10:10). Make Your voice of truth and direction (Isa 30:21) the loudest voice they hear.

Prayer to walk with You: Lord, please put someone in the path of every student to introduce Jesus to him or her. I want every child in my room to know the height, depth, and breadth of Your love (Eph 3:18). I pray that each student will taste and see that You are good (Ps 34:8) and that Your commands bring joy (Ps 19:8). I pray that each student will always seek You so that nothing good is lacking from his or her life (Ps 34:10).

REFLECTIONS

1. Ask God to show you anything that you might be taking for granted about your students. Journal what you sense God telling you.

2. Does praying for your students change your heart toward any of them? How?

3. Keep a record of how God answers your prayers for your kids this week. Write down anything you notice as evidence of God's power at work in your classroom.

SCRIPTURES

"What other nation is so great as to have their gods near them the way the LORD our God is near us when we pray to him?"

—Deuteronomy 4:7

"The LORD is righteous in all his ways and faithful in all he does. The LORD is near to all who call on him, to all who call on him in truth."

—Psalm 145:17–18

"Therefore I tell you, whatever you ask for in prayer, believe that you have received it, and it will be yours."

—Mark 11:24

Praying for Families
BE A BLESSING TODAY

• • • •

Three beautiful girls bounced out of their mother's car every morning at drop-off time. And every day, as each girl's feet touched the sidewalk, their mom called out, "Be a blessing to your teacher today!" And, of course, they all were. It was a beautiful family who served Jesus, raised children to be respectful and hard-working, and who looked for ways to make school folks feel appreciated and valued. Finding that family's last name on a class list was reason for the happy dance.

Your first thought is probably the same as mine. Wouldn't it be awesome if every parent was like that? Wouldn't this job be so much easier if all parents valued our work and instilled respect and appreciation in their children the way that mom did? Give me a class full of those parents' children, please!

The truth is that many parents we encounter do mirror that mom's expectations. In fact, part of the magic of this job is joining hands with parents and watching students grow when we work as a team on their behalf. The joy of that teamwork is part of what keeps us coming back each fall to try again.

But not all parents make our job easier, do they? We also serve families who, for whatever reason, struggle to parent in ways that support what we do at school. Many actively blame us for their child's problems or unrealistically expect us to fix what is broken. There are times and situations where parents simply make our work life difficult.

When a mom makes us famous on social media because her child's class party wasn't planned to her satisfaction, it distracts us. When a dad won't own his son's brokenness and blames us for his misbehavior, it demeans and discourages us. When parents won't accept boundaries and tell their child our rules are not important, it limits what we can accomplish each day. When grandparents, exhausted from raising two generations, can't get papers signed or forms returned on time, it wastes precious time. When estranged parents fight in the parking lot over who picks up the child, the sadness we feel for that child overwhelms us.

It is tempting to judge or criticize or even see difficult parents as the enemy. But, friends, we are all broken in some way, and parents suffer from the same brokenness that impacts the students we teach. The same enemy who fights for the hearts and minds of our students is fighting to destroy their families. Parents are divided by divorce, crippled by addictions, bound up by anxiety, and reeling from their own childhood traumas and unhealed wounds. So much pressure, so much comparison, so much pain.

This week, let's turn the tables on the real enemy. I know we would love a roomful of parents who know how to bless us, but let's be a blessing to them by lifting them up to the Lord. Let's take our inspiration from Hezekiah one more time and "go up to the temple of the LORD and spread it out before the LORD" (2 Kings 19:14) on behalf of all our parents. Let's fight for them on our knees this week because our students desperately need their families to experience the power and healing of our loving God.

Dear Enemy-Conquering Father,

Thank You for the parents You have entrusted to me this year—moms and dads, stepparents, aunts and uncles, grandparents and great-grandparents, adoptive parents, anyone who has taken on parenting responsibilities in the lives of my students. Lord, You see their hearts, their hurts, their struggles, and You love them all. Strengthen me with Your love so I can love them like You do. Father, please make a way for every parent in my class to have a relationship with You through Jesus. Allow Your Holy Spirit to lead them into truth and to show them Your will for their family. Where there is brokenness, restore and refresh. Where there is conflict, whisper peace. Where there are wounds, forgive and heal. Where there is regret and shame, breathe out hope. Where there is exhaustion from the struggle, provide rest. Break chains of addiction, heal generational scars, and overcome all work of the enemy in the families of my students. In Jesus' name, Amen.

REFLECTIONS

1. What specific issues are your students facing related to family brokenness? How can you pray for those families this week?

2. As you pray for your most difficult family situations, does God change your heart toward anyone in that family? How?

3. Journal ways God answers your prayers for the parents of your students this week.

SCRIPTURES

"As for me, far be it from me that I should sin against the LORD by failing to pray for you. And I will teach you the way that is good and right."

—1 Samuel 12:23

"May the Lord direct your hearts into God's love and Christ's perseverance."

—2 Thessalonians 3:5

"For the eyes of the Lord are on the righteous and his ears are attentive to their prayer, but the face of the Lord is against those who do evil."

—1 Peter 3:12

Praying for Colleagues
I'M PRAYING FOR HER

• • • •

A colleague's ill-advised choices suddenly made school life difficult for all of us and spawned a frenzy of gossip and division. Most of us lost our focus. Whispered conversations sent us to our computers to email a friend on the next hallway. Impromptu gatherings in the parking lot became our venue for replaying the colleague's shortcomings. Nighttime phone conversations fed the frenzy until many of us spent more time bashing that poor colleague than we did teaching our students.

I noticed, though, that one of my teammates didn't participate in the gossip. She remained steadfast in her refusal to make disparaging comments about our colleague even when the rest of us talked about little else. "Even if what you are saying about her is true," she told our team, "you are not helping anything by repeating it." Stung by her comment and a little indignant, I asked what she was doing to help. "I'm praying for her," she said quietly. "I'm praying for all of us."

I'm so thankful God puts people in our path who rise above the craziness and model sanity for the rest of us. Through that precious colleague's wisdom and courage, God began to whisper convicting questions to my spirit. Why wasn't I praying for my colleague in trouble? Why wasn't I praying for all my colleagues? Why was I choosing gossip over compassion? Why was I focusing on what she did wrong instead of asking God to help her make the right choice? Why was I adding to a fellow teacher's burden when we all needed each other's support to do this job? Why wasn't I asking for God's guidance and healing in my school so we could do what we were there to do?

God had my attention. I knew He was calling me higher, inviting me to participate in His plan to restore hope and peace and purpose in our school. I knew He wanted me to stop criticizing and start praying, but more questions came. What do I pray? How do I pray for colleagues when I don't agree with what they've done? How will my prayers make a difference?

Maybe God is whispering some of the same questions to your spirit. Maybe He is inviting you to rise above the chaos and trust Him to restore peace and purpose in your school family. Maybe you have some of the same questions about what to pray and where to find time and inspiration. Like He often does, God provided my answers in the pages of Scripture. Maybe what I found will inspire you to pray for the folks who work alongside you each day.

The Apostle Paul wrote a beautiful prayer for his fellow workers. He had experienced the challenges of his own calling, and he knew that those in the middle of the fight, those struggling every day to make a difference for Jesus (you know, people like us), were called to a mission they could only accomplish through the power of God. Listen to his prayer for his colleagues in the Colossian church:

For this reason, since the day we heard about you, we have not stopped praying for you. We continually ask

God to fill you with the knowledge of his will through all the wisdom and understanding that the Spirit gives, so that you may live a life worthy of the Lord and please him in every way: bearing fruit in every good work, growing in the knowledge of God, being strengthened with all power according to his glorious might so that you may have great endurance and patience, and giving joyful thanks to the Father, who has qualified you to share in the inheritance of his holy people in the kingdom of light (Colossians 1:9–12).

Short, complete, and life-giving. I would love to know a colleague somewhere was praying those words over me, wouldn't you? What if we started praying for one another using Paul's model? What if we could rise above the distractions and ask God to do for our colleagues what Paul asked Him to do for his coworkers in the faith? What if, instead of whispering about our colleagues to others we whispered Paul's prayer to God for them instead? Would we see God empower those in our profession the way He did the believers Paul prayed for?

I witnessed the school-changing power of prayer from my courageous teammate who simply made the decision to talk to God on behalf of her colleagues. Her prayers inspired others to pray, and as we prayed, God began to heal our school family. He opened our eyes to solutions. He restored peace and focus. He changed lives. Miracles happened, and it all started with one person's decision to pray.

Our calling to teach is a mission far greater than any of us can do alone. We need each other. We need the power of God bringing hope and victory to weary colleagues. We need His strength to touch the lives of the people who work alongside us. We need to remember that when one of us falls, we all suffer. When one of us overcomes, we are all strengthened. We are family. Not every colleague is a close friend. Not every colleague has the same teaching style. Not every colleague makes great decisions all the time, but every colleague is a member of the school family, and our family needs our prayers.

Dear Prayer-Answering Father,

Please give me a heart to pray for my colleagues. Remind me that Your power changes lives. I can't even think of a prayer better than the one You provided for me in Colossians, so I will rephrase Paul's words. This week, Lord, I pray that each one of my colleagues will:

1. Know Your will in every situation
2. Be filled with Your wisdom
3. Please You in everything they do
4. Accomplish great things (bear fruit)
5. Be strengthened with Your power
6. Do their work with endurance
7. Live in joy
8. Have a thankful heart

In Jesus' name, Amen.

REFLECTIONS

1. What are some of the situations in your own school that make you aware of the need to pray for your colleagues?

2. What question is God whispering to your heart about praying for your colleagues?

3. As you pray this week, notice and journal any ways God changes your own heart and how He answers your prayers for your co-workers.

SCRIPTURES

"Then Jesus told his disciples a parable to show them that they should always pray and not give up."

—Luke 18:1

"The end of all things is near. Therefore be alert and of sober mind so that you may pray. Above all, love each other deeply, because love covers over a multitude of sins."

—1 Peter 4:7–8

"Devote yourselves to prayer, being watchful and thankful."

—Colossians 4:2

Praying for Leaders
WE'VE COME TO PRAY FOR YOU

• • • •

Caring for aging parents is one of the toughest jobs ever. Couple that with any job in education, and the struggle is real. I had just returned to full-time work as a principal. My eighty-year-old mother, already on dialysis three days a week and needing a high level of care, was told she needed open heart surgery the day before teachers returned to start a new school year. She faced daunting challenges, and my siblings and I faced days and nights at the hospital and a new level of caregiving when she came home. I had no idea how I would manage my share of responsibility in her care and get school opened and ready for a new year.

Sitting at my desk the day after her surgery, my spirit was exhausted and overwhelmed. I looked up to see three teachers standing in my doorway. "We've come to pray for you." One of them walked around my desk, took my hand, and led me the few steps to their circle where they held hands and prayed that God would give me the wisdom and strength to walk through the season I faced.

The feeling of peace and love that washed over me when those beautiful prayer warriors went to God on my behalf is difficult to articulate. Through the prayers of His obedient saints, God unleashed strength and wisdom to lead, even in the middle of a challenging personal season.

I was a blessed leader. The prayers of teachers sustained me through many difficult times, and I felt God's power working in our school, far beyond anything I could accomplish. Yet, even though I experienced first-hand the mighty power of God through the prayers of those I led, I wasn't always as unselfish in praying for my own leaders. I did pray for them. For some of them. For those who inspired me. For those whose policies made sense to me. But the ones who didn't lead the way I wanted were often the subject of my silent criticism or voiced complaints to others instead of my faithful prayer for God's will to be done through their leadership.

My own attitude toward praying for leaders mirrored the current culture where we give ourselves permission to respect authority only when we agree with that person's policies, politics, or personal lifestyle, but God calls us higher than that. He reminds us in Romans 13:1 that "There is no authority except that which God has established. The authorities that exist have been established by God." Every leader has been appointed to his or her position for a divine purpose. And His instructions for praying for them are clear. "I urge, then, first of all, that petitions, prayers, intercession and thanksgiving be made for all people—for kings and all those in authority, that we may live peaceful and quiet lives in all godliness and holiness" (1 Tim 2:1–2).

God doesn't discriminate in His instruction to us for praying for leaders. He says *all* those in authority. For us that means school administrators, school leadership teams, central office staff, school boards, school directors, even elected officials who set the policies our local leaders must abide by. Whether policies make sense. Whether decisions seem wise. Whether we agree with lifestyle. School leadership is a tough assignment, and God is the only answer. Calling out to Him in prayer for our leaders to follow His guidance is our best hope for inspired leadership.

We pray for our leaders because God tells us to. We pray because we need God to pour out His power in the lives of our leaders so that our profession can be refreshed and renewed. And we pray because God, in His love for us, attaches a sweet promise for us when we obey. He promises a more peaceful life, marked by godliness and holiness.

Join me in praying for leaders this week. You don't have to literally take them by the hand like my teachers did (although that would be amazing), you can lift them quietly in your heart or join with like-minded friends. But this week, let's go to God on behalf of all our leaders. Let's lift them up to the God who has a divine purpose for each. Let's rest in the peace He promises as we look to heaven and say, "Father, I've come to pray for them."

Dear Leader-Anointing Father,

Thank You for those You have put in positions of authority. I don't always understand Your purpose, but I understand Your call to me to pray for all of them. I pray for every leader I serve to have a relationship with You through Jesus. I pray that each one will seek You and hear You and follow Your voice. Fill my leaders with Your wisdom and reveal to them that their greatest calling is to serve You by serving those under their authority. Give them Your strength and anoint them for leadership. Help them pursue peace in dealing with those they serve. Grant them rest for their souls and strengthen them for the important work of school leadership. I lift my leaders to You because You are the source of power for our profession, and You can bring hope and healing in ways I cannot imagine. I trust Your power to work in the leadership of my school. In Jesus' name, Amen.

REFLECTIONS

1. Find time to spend with God this week praying for your leaders. Ask Him to show you specific ways you can pray for each one.

2. Did praying for your leaders bring peace to your own heart this week? Do you notice more godliness in you?

3. Be aware of how God answers your prayers this week as you pray for your leaders. Journal what you notice.

SCRIPTURES

"If my people, who are called by my name, will humble themselves and pray and seek my face and turn from their wicked ways, then I will hear from heaven, and I will forgive their sin and will heal their land."
—2 Chronicles 7:14

"You will seek me and find me when you seek me with all your heart."
—Jeremiah 29:13

"Let your gentleness be evident to all. The Lord is near. Do not be anxious about anything, but in every situation, by prayer and petition, with thanksgiving, present your requests to God.
—Philippians 4:5–6

Praying for Our Profession
ESTABLISH THE WORK OF OUR HANDS

• • • •

An old friend sat across the dinner table listening to my stories about work. She had left teaching many years earlier and was always interested in hearing what was going on in the world of education. That week had been a tough one, and as I told her as much as I could legally disclose about situations I had faced that week, she just shook her head and chuckled when I stopped to take a breath. "You're making this up," she said. "I know you're making this up."

We both knew I wasn't. The stories were real. The problems were real, but to someone outside the profession, the complexity of what we face on a daily basis can be difficult to comprehend. I was able to share a chuckle at the absurdity of it all, but deep inside, my heart gasped at the enormity of energy required of me to address each issue that week. Her comment brought fresh questions to my own heart about whether I was really making a difference or just putting out fires. Hopelessness settled in my heart after that conversation, and I began to question the value of my work.

You face many of the same challenges. Challenges that are difficult to believe if you don't live them every day. Challenges that are taking their toll on our profession. We chose this work. We love what we do. We embrace the unique and complex challenges we face each day. But our profession is becoming more and more burdened, and good teachers are leaving in record numbers. Many who stay become discouraged or disgruntled. Where we used to experience deep satisfaction in the purpose and meaning of our work, we often wonder if we are making a difference at all.

We know that we have been called to this work. We heard God speak our name and lovingly call us to play a part in His eternal plan through the work we do. We understand that our heart's deep desire for our life's work to have value and meaning was put there by our Father. But that doesn't mean we don't experience times when we question the value of what we do. It doesn't mean we don't feel despair when our work no longer fills our desire to make a difference in the world.

The deep cry of our heart for our work to have lasting value and meaning is not a new cry. That desire is mirrored in Moses' prayer in Psalm 90, the oldest Psalm in the Bible: "May the favor of the Lord, our God rest upon us; establish the work of our hands for us—yes, establish the work of our hands" (v 17). Moses cried out to God to give his life's work lasting meaning. Moses, the man who watched God part the ocean so two million people could walk a dusty path to freedom, questioned whether any of his effort would outlive the desert. Moses, the man whose eyes watched the hand of God write the Ten Commandments on rocks, wondered whether his ministry would have eternal value. Yes, the same man who saw crazy miracles also experienced great questions about whether his work would ultimately make a difference. He had poured his life into a generation of stubborn, rebellious, entitled people who never quite grasped his teaching.

But Moses did what we must do. He prayed. He cried

out to the One who empowered his work and established it to reach into the future and inspire us three thousand years later. I believe God wants to do the same for our profession. Will you join me this week in fervent prayer that teachers all over our country will turn to God, ask Him to establish the work of their hands, and trust Him to give their work the meaning and value they so deeply desire?

Dear Value-Establishing Father,

You are not surprised by our desire to make a difference because You put it there. You are not challenged by the questions about the value of our work. You know what we face. Many days, it seems that our efforts are in vain, but we know that You have the power to take what we do and give it lasting value. Even though we may not always see the end result of our efforts, God, we trust You, and we believe that You will touch eternity through the work of our hands. In Jesus' name, Amen.

REFLECTIONS

1. Spend time with God this week asking Him to reveal where you have lost your faith in the power of your ministry. Write down what you hear.

2. In what way does it relieve stress to believe God will establish the work of your hands? How does it give you hope? Does it change the way you look at difficulties?

3. When you ask God to "establish the work of our hands," what exactly are you asking Him to do? What does that mean to you? Do you believe that God will do it?

SCRIPTURES

"I know that there is nothing better for people than to be happy and do good while they live. That each of them may eat and drink, and find satisfaction in all their toil—this is the gift of God."

—Ecclesiastes 3:12–13

"Whatever you do, work at it with all your heart, as working for the Lord, not for human masters, since you know that you will receive an inheritance from the Lord as a reward. It is the Lord Christ you are serving."

—Colossians 3:23–24

"God is not unjust; he will not forget your work and the love you have shown him as you have helped his people and continue to help them."

—Hebrews 6:10

Acknowledgments

Jerry, you are my man! You are my rock and my best friend, and my love and respect for you grow with every day we spend together. Your strength and your tenacious love for our blended family inspire and encourage me, and your unwavering faith helps me keep my focus on Jesus. Thank you for loving and believing in me, thank you for leading our family with integrity and godly courage, and thank you for always finding a way to make me laugh. I love you with all my heart and I am so proud to call you my husband.

Lindsay, you are my precious daughter, sister in Christ, and trusted friend. Thank you for the hours of listening to my ideas, for your faithful prayers, for reminding me of God's truth when I get off track, and for your unwavering belief in my calling to write. It is a deeply appreciated blessing to be your mom, and I fully expect to see your own book in print someday…soon.

Will and Meredith, I couldn't be more grateful that you are in my life. Thank you for always choosing to see the best in me, for your devotion to our family, and for raising children who love God and inspire me daily. Even though we don't share blood, you are my family, and I am so thankful to do life with you and the kids.

Angie, you are a gift from the heart of God. I have treasured your friendship and your family for many years and through many seasons of our lives. Your faithful prayers and sweet encouragement have often lifted me up to see possibilities I could have never imagined without you. This book is one of those possibilities. I owe you so much, and I pray that someday I can repay all the kindness you have shown me.

Lorrie, from bagel bites to windy beach trips to back-up cameras and beyond, our friendship has spanned almost thirty years and more life seasons than we can count. The laughs and tears we have shared together are some of my most precious memories, and your courage to walk through difficult times with faith has been a model of strength and perseverance more times than you realize.

My friends Sheri, Karan, Vicki, Mandy, and Chet, thank you for embracing the vision for this book from the beginning. Your input helped shape the outcome, and your encouragement along the way was a lifeline when discouragement and doubt threatened this dream. I have been privileged to work alongside you and deeply admire the work you do in your schools every day. I cherish each one of you as colleagues and friends.

Laci, your courage and fierce pursuit of your dreams inspired me from the moment I met you. Thank you for opening the door to a closer relationship with the Father and for teaching me to recognize His voice and His presence. As I wrote most of these devotions in the "cottage," the many prayers you lifted up there echoed through my heart.

Natalie, I had no idea what I was doing when I started this project, but God brought you into the process early, and you have been a patient and gentle guide. Thank you for your expertise and for your heart to help me encourage teachers through the power of God's word. What a blessing you have been throughout this process.

Sweet Mama Jean, you have prayed for this book every

single day since I shared the dream with you. Thank you for being a faithful prayer warrior and friend and for all those times around your table when we received so much more than physical nourishment. We have only been in each other's lives a few short years, but our friendship is an eternal one. I love you.

My colleagues through the years, thank you for what you taught me about teaching. Thank you for the creative ways you helped students learn. Thank you for all the ways you modeled God's grace to others. Thank you for continuing to learn and grow and find new ways to connect with the hearts of your students. Thank you for the belly laughs we shared, the tears we cried, and the stories we know are true, even if nobody else believes they really happened.

Dear Teacher Friends,

I am honored that you walked through these devotions with me. Thank you for allowing me to reminisce and be amazed all over again at how passionately I still love this profession and how present God has been in my own teaching journey.

I hope you know that I pray for you all often. I have seen teaching become more and more difficult over the past few years, and I know that many days leave you desperate for a new touch from God. I will continue to pray that God's power and love touch your work every day and give you fresh joy and greater strength to do His work.

What you do is important. It has a profound impact on our culture and eternal impact for the kingdom of God. Even when it isn't fully acknowledged or adequately compensated, your work matters.

I pray that you will continue to allow God to nourish your teacher heart with His Word. I pray that you believe you are loved and chosen, that you were never meant to fight your battles alone, and that God will give you everything you need to do your work. I pray that you find honor and dignity in your assignment and that God exceedingly and abundantly does more than you could ever imagine.

I pray that your classes are filled with students who want to learn, whose parents are supportive and kind to you, and whose lives reflect the influence you so lovingly pour into them.

I pray that you work with dedicated, creative and hard-working colleagues.

I pray that your leaders serve with integrity and inspiration.

I pray that our amazing profession will be transformed through the power of God in you.

I pray that your work reaches into the future to inspire and transform lives long after God tells you it's time to retire.

God bless the hearts of teachers everywhere.

Made in the USA
Monee, IL
14 August 2023

41024957R00090